MW00595419

HISTORY OF JAZZ

Lecture Notes • Overheads • Listening Examples

Tom Collier

KENDALL/HUNT PUBLISHING COMPANY
4050 Westmark Drive   Dubuque, Iowa 52002

Cover clip art by Click ART The Instant Image Resource.

Contents

Preface

History Of Jazz: Lecture Notes, Overheads, and Listening Examples is not intended to be used as a formal textbook, but rather, a useful resource of information for students taking a college or university level course in jazz history. Much of this manual is written in outline form and mirrors the style of lecture and overhead projector notes commonly used by instructors to deliver the important elements of jazz history in a lecture classroom situation. Used in conjunction with formal textbooks such as Mark Gridley's *Jazz Styles*, Frank Tirro's *Jazz: A History*, or Lewis Porter and Michael Ullman's *Jazz, From Its Origins To The Present*, this collection of data can be a useful supplement for a student studying jazz history.

History Of Jazz: Lecture Notes, Overheads, and Listening Examples emerged from a ten-week, 3-credit course (meeting three days a week) that I teach at the University Of Washington for mostly non-music major students, *The History Of Jazz*. Unfortunately, due to the limited time factor in teaching 100 years of jazz history in 30, one-hour class meetings, many important musicians and contributors to jazz have been left out in favor of the most influential and pivotal figures. The omission of such jazz luminaries as Clark Terry, Mary Lou Williamson, Stan Kenton, Gerry Mulligan, Art Blakey, Sun Ra, Chick Corea and others, was a difficult decision, but necessary considering the incredible amount of information that must be presented within the confines of the university quarter system. On the positive side, this manual cuts to the most essential information necessary for a solid base of understanding of jazz history and the musicians who helped to shape it the most.

The fourteen units comprising this manual can be comfortably presented in a typical ten week quarter. I use the following schedule:

Week 1:	1. Introduction	Week 6:	7. Modern Jazz - Bebop
	2. Roots of Jazz - blues	Week 7:	8. Cool Jazz
Week 2:	2. Roots of Jazz, ragtime, etc.		9. Hard Bop
	3. Early Jazz - New Orleans	Week 8:	10. Miles Davis
Week 3:	3. Early Jazz, conclusion	Week 9:	11. John Coltrane
	4. Chicago Jazz		12. Avant-Gard/Free Jazz
Week 4:	5. Stride Piano	Week 10:	13. Jazz Rock/Fusion
	6. The Swing Era, part 1		14. Neoclassicism / Post-
Week 5:	6. The Swing Era, part 2		Modern Bop
	Midterm Exam	Week 11:	Final Exam (Finals Week)

The information contained within has been compiled with the notion that students using this manual have not had a great deal of formal musical training, or personal involvement with jazz music. Jazz theory, in-depth musical analysis, and other technical "music-major stuff" has been kept to an absolute minimum in favor of a more direct style of communication intended for a novice student of jazz. For instance, the 83 listening examples in this manual contain information and terminology that is intended to spark the student's interest in the music, not drive a wedge through the listening process. After all, one of the primary goals of a good jazz history course is to go beyond introducing a new musical style to a classroom of students, but to ensure that a majority of them will become life-long listeners of jazz.

I. Lecture Notes and Overheads

1. Introduction

The primary element of jazz is improvisation; the art of simultaneously composing and performing music.

The Three Universal Elements of Music

1. Melody

The tune; the lead vocal or instrumental line; lead singers or lead instrumentalists play melodies, or melodic lines. In most instances, improvisation in music is the instant creation and performance of melodic lines.

2. Harmony

Usually involves the accompaniment to the melody, or a counter line to the melody such as a backup singer in pop music or a walking bass line in jazz. Harmony is the movement of **CHORDS:** A chord is three or more notes sung or played simultaneously, or in rapid order: the piano, guitar, and vibes are capable of playing chords; multiple singers or instrumentalists can play chords as a group such as a saxophone section in a jazz band, or the backup singers in a doo-wop vocal group.

3. Rhythm

Rhythm involves many sophisticated elements, the most basic being the pace, or pulse, of the notes. Most people feel rhythm through drumming patterns, although the bass and rhythm guitar also provide additional rhythmic energy in jazz or popular music.

Pulse or **TEMPO:** the speed of the music (slow......fast).

BEAT(S): rhythmic patterns are divided into beats; probably 95% of all popular and jazz music contains rhythmic patterns divided into 4-beat patterns. An example of popular music that is **NOT** divided into 4-beat patterns would be the waltz, whose rhythmic patterns are based upon a division of 3.

MEASURE or **BAR:** a grouping of beats constitutes a measure, or bar (both terms mean exactly the same thing in music). If the rhythm is based upon 4-beat patterns, then a measure would contain 4 beats. Within a measure, there are strong and weak beats: the strongest beats falls on the first and third beats of a measure (based upon 4-beat patterns), while the weak beats fall on two and four.

SYNCOPATION: one of the most important elements of jazz, syncopation involves stressing the weak beats rather than the strong beats in a measure resulting in rhythmic tension; complex syncopation involves stressing beats in-between the four primary beats (in a 4-beat rhythmic pattern).

SWING FEEL: next to improvisation, the swing feel in jazz is the most distinctive characteristic of the music; the manner of swing depends on the complexity of syncopation.

3

2. Roots of Jazz

- Blues
- Ragtime
- Brass Bands

I. The Blues

Roots of the Blues

FIELD HOLLERS: sung by solitary workers in the fields.

WORK SONGS: sung by a group of workers, usually with a tool of labor such as a pick, axe, hammer, or shovel.

RELIGIOUS SONGS: provided a positive look at life after slavery; hope for heavenly rewards. The form of the blues came primarily from religious hymns sung by the slaves.

Country or Rural Blues

BLUES FORM - **A - A - B**; derived from (Baptist) hymns

lyric form: A: statement of problem, feeling, situation, etc.

  A: repeat of the above, sometimes with additional words

  B: response to the A statement (solution, moral message, etc.)

music form: A: I chord = home key

  A: IV chord resolving to the I chord

  B: V chord resolving to the I chord

City or Urban Blues

❑ **A - A - B** form formally structured into three 4-bar phrases = **12-bar blues**
❑ vocal style related to European "trained" vocal techniques, e.g. the use of a steady **vibrato,** less "liquid" in quality than southern singers and clearer enunciation of words
❑ powerful vocal style; blues singers in the cities sang in noisy bars as well as the large Vaudeville theaters without microphone amplification
❑ vocalist accompanied by a band (ensemble approach) rather than the solitary folk singing style of country blues; often, the vocalist engaged in call & response with a featured horn soloist in the band
❑ lyrics were more sophisticated and dealt with universal themes of love, freedom, etc. instead of the local, or regional themes of country blues

Comparison of Country Blues & Urban Blues

	Country Blues	**Urban Blues**
Lyric themes	local events, people; love, death, freedom	universal themes urban life, relationships; political, etc.
song structures	A - A - B; 3 unequal phrases	(verse) - A - A - B; three 4-bar phrases (12-bar blues)
vocal style	raw, nasal vocal sound; lots of vocal effects such as bent notes, scoops, smears; "liquid" quality	refined, full vocal sound; use of vibrato; restrained vocal effects; accurate pitches; less "liquid"
accompaniment	folk singing style; self-accompaniment on guitar or banjo	ensemble approach; lead vocal accompanied by a band
performers	itinerant male folk singers traveling the rural South	predominantly female vaudeville singers performing in larger clubs and theaters in metropolitan areas

Blues and Jazz

❑ blues is one of the roots of jazz

- basis for improvisation
- provided a standard repertoire of songs
- introduced blues notes
- instrumentalists used vocal inflections (scoops, smears, bent notes, etc.) in order to "sing through their horns"
- provided jazz with soul

❑ blues has maintained its identity separate from jazz
❑ jazz musicians must be able to play the blues; blues musicians are not required to play jazz

II. Ragtime

❑ ragtime is generally NOT considered a style of jazz since the music lacks improvisation, the most striking feature of jazz
❑ however, many of ragtime's musical characteristics can be heard in the first jazz recordings
❑ ragtime was thoroughly composed for the piano (the home entertainment center of the 1890's)

right hand (melody): syncopated melodic lines usually based upon 3-note patterns

left hand (harmony & rhythm): march-like rhythms based upon 2-beat patterns

❏ the term ragtime can be traced to three primary sources:

1. dance

   • popular 19th century exaggerated black dance style was referred to as a rag dance, or ragging; high leg kicks, wide arm movements, limber torso twists

2. improvisation

   • early jazz musicians used the dance term to describe melodic paraphrasing of existing tunes; an early word for jazz improvisation:

"I remember 'ragging' light classical numbers"
—Jelly Roll Morton, early jazz pianist

3. rhythm

   • the rhythmic feel of the music felt "ragged" with the left hand playing 2-beat march-like patterns against the syncopated, three-note melodic patterns of the right hand

❏ The most important and influential ragtime composer was **Scott Joplin** (1868–1917), born in Bowie County, Texas

❏ **Scott Joplin's** ragtime pieces and their syncopated rhythms influenced the development of early jazz playing styles more than any other rags

Ragtime and Jazz

❏ ragtime provided early jazz groups their first repertoire of non-blues tunes on which the musicians could improvise

❏ early jazz horn players borrowed ragtime (right-hand) melodic phrasing ideas

❏ early jazz rhythm section players (piano bass, drums, banjo) emulated the left-hand march patterns (the first jazz bands were marching bands)

❏ early jazz musicians borrowed the idea of multiple simultaneous melodies, or counterpoint in arranging ragtime pieces for their bands

III. New Orleans and Brass Bands

New Orleans was the social, economic, and political focal point of the South after the Civil War; all roads and railroads converged on the city along with ships from around the world making New Orleans a prosperous, vibrant city of blending cultures. New Orleans was a unique city, particularly for blacks:

■ even before the Civil War, some blacks enjoyed certain freedoms and privileges unavailable in the rest of the south:

   • land ownership
   • slave ownership

■ before the Civil War, a caste system developed into three distinct groups:

1. free whites including Creoles (mixed black/French or black/Spanish)
2. free blacks
3. slaves

❑ Creoles and free blacks formed a tight-knit society in New Orleans featuring their own social clubs, businesses, and professional organizations
❑ many Creoles attended French schools and spoke French instead of English

■ formal classical music training was readily available; this elite society presented classical music concerts through their own organization known as the Negro Philharmonic Society
■ the center of this activity was east of Canal Street in the French Quarter of New Orleans

❑ on the flip side, black slaves lived in desperate poverty on the west side of Canal Street in the uptown area
❑ slaves were allowed to gather in Congo Square (Orleans and Rampart Streets) to sing and dance on certain weekends and holidays; Congo Square became a tourist attraction after the civil war

After the Civil War:

■ racial tensions increased
■ in 1894, city government created the **Black Codes**

1. anyone of African descent, including Creoles, were considered black
2. Creoles dropped to the bottom of the caste system - resented by the former slaves and ousted from their elite status by whites

■ Creoles were forced out of the French Quarter into desperate poverty in uptown, despised by all

Storyville

❑ by 1897, New Orleans was plagued by prostitution activity; city alderman Sidney Story proposed a licensed prostitution district which was approved that year:

■ named Storyville
■ located in uptown section
■ 38 city square blocks containing well over 200 brothels
■ main thoroughfare was Bourbon Street

❑ Storyville was divided into two sections:

1. White Storyville
2. **black Storyville** or **"Back O'Town"** - became the center of jazz activity

❑ Storyville is known today as the **"cradle of jazz"** - where New Orleans jazz was born

Brass Bands in Storyville

Most of the musicians in the Storyville brass bands were classically-trained Creole musicians, forced out of the concert halls of the French Quarter into the streets and brothels of Storyville.

❑ New Orleans **funeral parades** - an important ceremonial and social event in New Orleans:

 ■ solemn procession to the funeral site (slow hymns & spirituals)
 ■ up-tempo, happy marches & ragtime pieces on the way back to town

   • spontaneous arrangements of songs (improvisation)
   • lively, swinging march rhythms

❑ a few black New Orleans marching bands joined forces with ragtime piano players and blues singers at night in the brothels, bars and clubs of Storyville and surrounding neighborhoods

 ■ horn players learned the intricacies of ragtime and the soul of the blues
 ■ ragtime pianists learned the art of improvisation

3. Early Jazz - New Orleans Style

The First Jazz Bands

❑ the term **"jazz"** came from the streets of black Storyville; slang for sexual activity

❑ during the 1930's, **Jelly Roll Morton** recalled another meaning for the term:

■ short for *jasmine,* a major spice import into New Orleans; **"we were spicing-up the music - you know, jassin' it up"**; it is true that many early bands spelled jazz with the two s's - jass

❑ early important Storyville brothel/jazz bands included:

■ Onward Brass Band
■ Olympia Brass Band
■ Excelsior Jass Band
■ Creole Jazz Band
■ Preservation Hall Jass Band

Buddy Bolden (186?-1931) - cornet

❑ the first important jazz musician and improviser
❑ he was a powerful cornetist with a high level of technique - unusual for black Storyville musicians

....
"You could hear Buddy Bolden's trumpet five miles away!"
—Louis Armstrong, Storyville jazz musician
....

❑ he set the early standards of jazz improvisation excellence
❑ suffered mental breakdown in 1907 and never played music in public again
❑ no recordings of Buddy Bolden exist

In 1917, bowing to pressure from the Department of Navy, New Orleans officially "shut-down" Storyville effectively ending significant employment of jazz musicians. With World War I on the horizon and employment opportunities opening up in the shops and factories in the northern cities, a large number of blacks migrated from their homes in the South and took up residencies in Chicago, Kansas City, New York, and other metropolitan areas. Jazz musicians, looking for new employment opportunities, found waiting audiences, especially in Chicago, New York, and Kansas City.

• No recordings of original Storyville jazz bands exist •

The First Jazz Recordings

Very few recordings of black performers exist prior to 1920:

- James Reese Europe and his Society Orchestra (1914-1917)
- W.C. Handy recorded several original compositions in 1917
- Bert Williams was the most popular black entertainer in vaudeville and made a few recordings prior to 1920

The first jazz recording was made in 1917 by a group of white New Orleans musicians led by cornetist **Nick LaRocca.** the band was known as **The Original Dixieland Jass Band** and for several years, their records were the only available jazz recordings. They gained widespread popularity and helped to popularize jazz in the United States and Europe, where they toured triumphantly after World War I. However, after the first recordings of original black New Orleans jazz musicians were released in the early 1920's, The Original Dixieland Jass Band faded into memory and by 1925, had disbanded.

Joe "King" Oliver and the Creole Jazz Band

Joe "King" Oliver (1885-1938) - cornet; took over from Buddy Bolden as the "King of Jazz" in New Orleans; remained the most significant and popular jazz musician until Storyville closed in 1917. Between 1914-1917, he tutored a young musician named **Louis Armstrong** offering him the work that he (Oliver) couldn't take.

1918 - migrated to Chicago and worked in bars and clubs with various bands

1921 - formed his own band and moved to San Francisco becoming the first significant New Orleans musician to play on the west coast

1922 - returned to Chicago and re-formed his old band, The Creole Jazz Band; invited his young protégé, Louis Armstrong (still living in New Orleans), to join the band

1923 - a Chicago black-owned record company, **Okeh Records,** known at that time as a **"race label,"** signed Oliver and the Creole Jazz Band to a recording contract

Louis Armstrong (1901-1971)

❑ born into desperate poverty in the "Back O'Town" of Storyville on August 4, 1901
❑ his birth certificate was lost until 1991 and throughout his life, he used July 4, 1900, as his birth date because "it was an all-American birth date"

....

"If the least successful of the masterpieces he created in the late 1920's with his Hot Five and Hot Seven were the only available example of Armstrong's art, it would still be regarded as a unique and monumental jazz milestone."

—Ira Gitler, jazz historian

....

❑ 1925-1929: Armstrong formed a new jazz band at the request of Okeh Records; **The Hot Five,** featured former members of the Creole Jazz Band:

- Louis Armstrong - cornet
- Johnny Dodds - clarinet
- Kid Ory - trombone
- Lil (Hardin) Armstrong - piano
- Johnny St. Cyr - banjo

- the band signed a record contract with Chicago's Okeh Records in 1925 and their recordings over the next few years revolutionized jazz - artistically and commercially
- the Hot Five were a recording band; their only live performance occurred in 1926 at a record industry convention in Chicago at the request of their label, Okeh Records; hence, the lack of a drummer in the band

Armstrong's Important Contributions to Jazz & Popular Music

1. changed the focus of jazz performance from collective improvisation to solo improvisation
2. abandoned the "stiffness" of ragtime phrasing and defined the "art of swinging"
3. was the first jazz soloist to improvise melodic lines that could stand by themselves in terms of structure, form, and musical creativity
4. raised the level of virtuosity in jazz; he set new levels of technical and creative excellence in improvised music; he extended the vocabulary for jazz soloists
5. popularized jazz more than any other musician
6. influenced vocalists, popular and jazz, with his swinging phrasing techniques and scat singing style

Sidney Bechet (1897-1959) - clarinet / soprano sax

- one of the finest Storyville clarinetists, Bechet, a Creole, was a first-rate musician and creative improviser, second only to Armstrong in the New Orleans style
- after the close of Storyville in 1917, spent time in New York City before traveling to Europe in 1919
- unlike American audiences who looked at the music as a novelty, Europeans took it seriously and heaped great praise on Bechet who decided to make Paris his home

....

"There is an extraordinary clarinet virtuoso who is, it seems, the first of his race to have composed perfectly formed blues on the clarinet. I've heard two of them which he had elaborated at great length. They are equally admirable for their richness of invention, force of accent, and daring in novelty and the unexpected. Already they give the idea of a style, and their form was gripping, abrupt, harsh, with a brusque and pitiless ending like that of Bach's second Brandenburg Concerto. I wish to set down the name of this artist of genius: as for myself, I shall never forget it - it is Sidney Bechet."
—Ernest Ansermet - Swiss orchestra conductor, critic; *Revue Romande*, October 1919

....

Bechet, who performed often in the United States and made most of his recordings here, became a national hero in France - he was awarded the French Legion of Honor and a statue of Bechet was erected in Paris after his death in 1959. He introduced jazz to Europeans who immediately embraced the music as a new, vibrant musical art form; Europeans have historically appreciated jazz much more than Americans.

13

4. Chicago Jazz

❏ by 1925, three categories of jazz musicians were performing in Chicago:

    1. older white musicians who looked at jazz as a novelty
    2. transplanted black New Orleans musicians; Louis Armstrong, etc.
    3. young, white musicians who studied the New Orleans style, used Armstrong as their role model, and emerged with a new energy after 1925

❏ several young Chicago musicians would carry the jazz tradition into the swing era of the 1930's and 1940's as major "stars" of popular and jazz music including:

Benny Goodman - clarinet
Glenn Miller - trombone
Tommy Dorsey - trombone
Jimmy Dorsey - alto sax and clarinet
Gene Krupa - drums
Davey Tough - drums

A Comparison of New Orleans and Chicago Jazz Styles

	New Orleans	**Chicago**
Improvisation focus	prior to 1925: collective improvisation; after 1925: solo improvisation; collective improvisation utilized during the playing of the melody at the beginning and ending of a song	solo improvisation; collective improvisation used during the playing of the melody at the beginning and ending of a song
Primary influences	Buddy Bolden Joe "King" Oliver, **Louis Armstrong**	Louis Armstrong, **Bix Beiderbecke**
Primary melody played by:	cornet / trumpet	cornet / trumpet
High counter-melody played by:	clarinet	clarinet
Low counter-melody played by:	trombone	**saxophone**, trombone
Basic rhythmic feel	4-beat march-like drumming patterns (carried over from parade band traditions)	2-beat ragtime drum patterns; excellent for dancing (transition to swing era drumming)

❏ the most important contribution to jazz by the young Chicago musicians was the introduction of the saxophone, soon to become the "icon" instrument of jazz

Leon Bix Beiderbecke (1903-1931)

❏ born into a middle-class family in Davenport, Iowa; mother was a piano teacher
❏ considered a musical protégé as a youngster; learned to play the piano on his own
❏ rebelled against his piano teachers; preferred to improvise his own versions of classical music and popular songs
❏ his mother preferred the piano music of the Impressionistic French composers **Maurice Ravel** and **Claude Debussy**; their complex harmonies were implanted into the mind of young Beiderbecke
❏ heard **Louis Armstrong** on a riverboat docked in Davenport in 1919; greatly moved by the New Orleans jazz style - especially, the improvisation factor
❏ bought a cheap cornet, several **Original Dixieland Jass Band** records, and proceeded to teach himself how to play the instrument along with the records
❏ dropped out of school to play in local dance bands; developed unorthodox playing techniques on the cornet which resulted in:

  ■ a softer, subtle, less-brassy tone
  ■ limited range on the horn; effective only in the low and middle registers
  ■ made up for rapid facility on the horn by incorporating clever, syncopated placement of notes, and the use of longer, held tones (very unusual approach to the instrument)

❏ arrived in Chicago in 1924 and immediately became a force in the Chicago jazz scene; his unusual playing and soulful improvisations caught everyone's attention, including Louis Armstrong:

....

"Every note he blew was so beautiful. I like that *Singin' the Blues* record and things like that. Nobody else gonna blow like he did. I never did play that tune because of Bix. I didn't want anybody to mess with it."

— Louis Armstrong - 1970 radio interview
....

❏ Beiderbecke made many of his recordings with **C-melody saxophonist Frankie Trumbauer** and his Orchestra (the C-melody sax was a very unusual instrument)
❏ shortly after *Singin' the Blues* was made, popular bandleader Paul Whiteman offered employment to Trumbauer, Beiderbecke, and the Dorsey brothers
❏ the move to New York proved to be quite lucrative for everyone except Beiderbecke who was falling into the abyss of alcoholism
❏ while his playing reached an international audience with Whiteman, his use of alcohol increased as an insulation against the excessive commercialism of Whiteman's music

....

"Lots of cats tried to play like Bix. Ain't none of them play like him yet. He was a born genius, but they crowded him with too much love."

— Louis Armstrong, 1970 radio interview
....

A Comparison of Louis Armstrong and Bix Beiderbecke

	Armstrong	**Biederbecke**
Command of the cornet	excellent technique with full facility and range	unorthodox technique; limited facility and range
Usual playing range	middle to high	low to middle
Tone quality	big, full brassy tone	soft, subtle, less-brassy
Improvisatory character	outgoing, bluesy, "hot"	reflective, blues references, "cool"
Harmonic thinking	bluesy; contemporary	advanced; elements of impressionistic harmonic understanding (ahead of his time by 15 years)
Rhythmic conception	swinging; laid-back, relaxed feel; broke the bonds of ragtime phrasing	somewhat unsettled; closely tied to ragtime; ragtime phrasing
Influences	Buddy Bolden, Joe "King" Oliver	Louis Armstrong, Original Dixieland Jass Band, Maurice Ravel, Claude Debussy

5. Stride Piano

Read 80-103

Ferdinand "Jelly Roll" Morton (1890-1941) - piano / composer

❑ Creole jazz pianist, Morton traveled to Chicago by way of Texas, St. Louis and Kansas City between 1917-1923
❑ Morton boasted that he invented jazz in New Orleans in 1902; while he did not single-handedly invent jazz, he was most certainly the first piano player to "jazz-up" the written melodies of ragtime compositions, popular songs, and light classical pieces
❑ his style of piano playing became known as **New Orleans stride**
❑ **stride** refers to the "walking", or striding, left-hand bass line patterns improvised by Morton as counterpoint lines to support his right-hand melodies

James P. Johnson (1891-1955) - piano

❑ Johnson emerged in New York during the 1920's as the foremost practitioner of the **Harlem stride** piano style; he became known as the **"father of Harlem stride"**
❑ Harlem stride grew out of the New Orleans stride style taking on distinct characteristics that were the result of the competitive nature of the New York based players
❑ Harlem stride piano players challenged each other in well-advertised cutting contests to see who could play the fastest, most complex solos
❑ Harlem stride was faster, more melodically complex, and less reliant upon the blues tradition than New Orleans stride
❑ harmonically, Harlem stride pianists explored the complexity of whole-tone and diminished scales and chords found in French Impressionistic piano music
❑ rhythmically, Harlem Stride swung hard and was the forerunner to boogie woogie, which emerged in the 1930's (which led directly to rhythm blues and rock & roll)
❑ basically, **New Orleans stride** focused on the soulful, bluesy side of piano playing while **Harlem stride** was built around a hard driving energy requiring virtuosic technique and harmonic complexity

Earl "Fatha" Hines (1903-1983) - piano

❑ Hines came to Chicago from Pittsburgh in the mid-1920's
❑ he developed a **percussive approach** to piano playing that set him apart from the other stride players; he literally attacked the keys with such energy, that he often broke piano strings during his performances
❑ he also perfected an approach to playing melodic lines by **doubling the melody in octaves** (high and low note of the same pitch); his original intention for doing this was so that he could be heard above the band in live performances
❑ Hines also utilized **flowery classical embellishments** in his playing which gave his improvisations a sense of "class"; this appealed to the mostly white record buying public
❑ he possessed tremendous technique, but used it sparingly; his association with

Louis Armstrong in 1928 brought him closer to the bluesy approach of New Orleans stride.

Thomas "Fats" Waller (1904-1943) - piano / vocalist

❑ Waller was a **student of James P. Johnson**; he also played the organ for silent movies as a teenager
❑ besides being a talented jazz musician, Waller was an entertainer in the same mold as Louis Armstrong; he became the second most popular black entertainer of the 1930's performing in theaters, nightclubs, and appearing in several Hollywood movies
❑ Waller also became known as an important composer of popular songs including such classic tunes as *Honeysuckle Rose, Ain't Misbehavin', Squeeze Me* and dozens more
❑ as a jazz pianist, he was an important bridge from stride to swing; while he possessed tremendous technique, he also focused on carefully constructed, soulful performances
❑ the first use of the word "funky" in describing a musical style was a New York music critic describing Waller's music in 1932; Waller was truly the first "funky" musician

Meade "Lux" Lewis (1905-1964) - piano

❑ Lewis was the leading exponent of **boogie woogie**
❑ **boogie woogie** was a popular blues/jazz piano style of the 1930's that grew out of stride and later evolved into the rolling piano style of the early rock & roll era in the 1950's
❑ **boogie woogie** was characterized by its unique, driving **walking left-hand bass riffs**
❑ melodic improvisations in the **right hand** were **highly syncopated blues-based riffs** that were often repeated many times to build the intensity of the music

Art Tatum (1910-1956) - piano   *Oscar Peterson*

> "In any given field of artistic endeavor, there are invariably those individuals who, through exceptional skill and generous twists of fate, tower over their colleagues and exert an influence that endures long after them. Art Tatum is one of those individuals who possessed a piano style so unique and technique so awesome that it defies imitation."
>
> —Gene Lees, jazz critic, author

❑ legally blind, self-taught genius-pianist; he learned classical music as a youngster by listening to piano recordings and imitating what he heard
❑ went to New York in 1932 and became a sensation with his own 15-minute radio program
❑ won every cutting contest he entered; **Fats Waller** remarked one night in the club that he was playing, upon seeing Tatum enter, **"God is in the house."**
❑ **Vladimir Horowitz,** the famous Russian classical pianist, remarked that he would "...give anything to have Art Tatum's left hand facility..."
❑ despite his virtuosity, Tatum was never popular with the general public; his reputation was made within the music community and with dedicated jazz fans; he never toured outside of the United States and rarely played with other musicians

6. The Swing Era or Big Band Era

The Swing Era, or **Big Band Era,** was largely associated with the bands that played in large ballrooms for multitudes of dancers and **"jitterbugs."** Swing music represents the period in which jazz became America's popular music, roughly between 1930 and 1945. Several white jazz musicians, including Benny Goodman, Harry James, The Dorsey Brothers, and Glenn Miller, became popular superstars during the swing era sporting legions of fans, swooning girls, as well as the extensive press coverage that accompanies stardom.

❑ many of the big names in swing came out of the young Chicago school of jazz in the 1920's, learning their craft from Louis Armstrong and other New Orleans musicians
❑ swing music grew out of the 1920's as a combination of:

1. society bands (such as Paul Whiteman)
2. New Orleans, Kansas City, and Chicago jazz

❑ basically, the society bands began combining improvised jazz solos with written arrangements of popular songs; the jazz element livened-up the music and appealed to the younger generation
❑ **all swing bands played for dancing;** however, some bands emphasized the jazz tradition more than other bands:

1. **Sweet Bands** (sometimes called Mickey bands): utilized very little or no jazz improvisation in their music (Guy Lombardo, Ozzie Nelson, Lawrence Welk, etc.)
2. **Hot Bands**: preferred to feature jazz improvisation, loud, driving rhythm section, and exciting shout choruses (Benny Goodman, Count Basie, Duke Ellington, etc.)

❑ in the context of *jazz* history, we will look at a few of the important **hot bands** and their significant jazz soloists
❑ the primary activity in the development of swing music occurred in New York during the 1920's

NOTE: three terms that you should know:

1. **composer** - a creator of new music
2. **arranger** - one who takes existing music and writes it out for someone else to perform
3. **composer/arranger** - one who composes and then writes out the music for others to perform

Jelly Roll Morton and His Red Hot Peppers

❏ Jelly Roll Morton was the first significant jazz pianist
❏ Morton was also the first significant **jazz composer** with such early compositions like *King Porter Stomp, Mr. Jelly Lord, Dead Man Blues* and *Grandpa's Spells*
❏ in the mid-1920's, Morton organized a band to play his compositions that he skillfully scored on paper; his intentions were to **combine written and improvised jazz**
❏ he experimented with various **sound textures** by carefully combining different combinations of instruments
❏ Morton was one of the first to utilize the **string bass** in place of the traditional tuba as the bass instrument in his band; he transferred his "striding" left hand piano patterns to the string bass in creating the standard **walking bass lines** that are commonplace in contemporary jazz
❏ in keeping with the tradition of New Orleans and simultaneous multiple melodies, or counterpoint, Morton often wrote-out 3-part counterpoint lines for his band

Fletcher Henderson (1897-1952) - piano / band leader / arranger

Fletcher Henderson established the modern instrumentation of a swing band and set the early standards for arranging music that were still utilized 70 years later by contemporary big band arrangers and composers.

❏ majored in science in college, but earned a living accompanying blues singers in New York, most notably Ethel Waters
❏ began his writing career in vaudeville, scoring arrangements of blues songs for the show bands that accompanied blues singers
❏ formed his own band in 1923 utilizing the basic instrumentation that has survived for decades in big band music:

  ■ saxophone section of 4-5 players who "doubled" on clarinet
  ■ trombone section of 2-3 players
  ■ trumpet section of 3-4 players
  ■ rhythm section consisting of piano, string bass, guitar, and drums

❏ each section in the band had a featured soloist and a **"lead" player** (sometimes the same person) who dictated tone quality, phrasing, and other musical elements to the other members in the section
❏ in 1924, his featured trumpet soloist was **Louis Armstrong**
❏ in 1926 he featured the first virtuoso tenor saxophone soloist **Coleman Hawkins**
❏ because he could not handle the demand for his written arrangements, he hired another "schooled" composer/arranger, **Don Redman,** who expanded Henderson's ideas
❏ Henderson introduced several jazz band arranging techniques that live on into the 21st century including:

  ■ pitted the saxes against the brass in a call and response format
  ■ developed effective **block chord voicings** within a section
  ■ introduced the concept of **soli (plural of solo):** a section within the band playing as one instrument, either in unison or in block chord harmony with the lead player e.g. saxophone soli

■ introduced the **shout chorus** which took on two forms:

1. **tutti shout chorus** - the whole band played the same thing in unison or in **block harmony** with the lead melody
2. **call & response shout chorus** - saxes stating one riff with the brass responding with a second riff always building intensity in the music

Fletcher Henderson is known as the "Father of the Modern Big Band"; during the swing era, he was in great demand by many bandleaders to write arrangements for their ensembles; many of the swing era's greatest hits were arranged by Fletcher Henderson.

Benny Goodman (1909-1986) - clarinet / bandleader

❑ came out of the 1920's Chicago school of young jazz musicians
❑ traveled to New York in 1929 with Ben Pollack's band; worked for several years as a studio and show musician
❑ 1934 - befriended by John Hammond, the son of a wealthy patron of the New York Philharmonic
❑ Hammond set up Goodman's first big break: appearances on an **NBC radio** network music program entitled **"Let's Dance"**
❑ fueled by radio exposure, Hammond negotiated a record deal with Columbia Records and organized a cross-country national tour culminating at the Palomar Theater in Los Angeles
❑ that performance, broadcast nationally on NBC, revealed a young, fanatic audience who wildly cheered Goodman and his band
❑ Benny Goodman became an overnight superstar; he was hailed as the **"King of Swing"**
❑ in 1938, Hammond was finally able to convince the **Carnegie Hall** management in New York that a jazz concert would be as musically substantive as a symphony concert; Benny Goodman's band was the first non-classical ensemble to perform in Carnegie Hall

While maintaining his superstar status, Goodman never lost sight of the jazz tradition and never forgot the musicians who taught him how to play jazz in Chicago. Because of his popularity, he became the first bandleader to perform in public with an ensemble comprised of black and white musicians. He brought integration into the music business a full ten years before Jackie Robinson broke that barrier in sports.

❑ in 1935, he hired **Fletcher Henderson** on a full-time basis as his personal music arranger and part-time pianist
❑ in 1936, Goodman discovered vibraphonist **Lionel Hampton** in Los Angeles and asked him to join his quartet, a group that Goodman recorded with in addition to his big band
❑ in 1939, Goodman hired a young electric guitarist, **Charlie Christian,** who revolutionized guitar playing through his recordings with Goodman
❑ Goodman's small group recordings of the 1930's and 1940's are considered some of the finest jazz performances of the 20th century
❑ the small group recordings appealed to jazz and popular audiences:

■ popular audiences preferred the tight, arrangements played by the group which was often called **chamber jazz**

23

■ jazz audiences marveled over the brilliant, spontaneous improvisations by Goodman, Hampton and Christian

Goodman's Legacy to Jazz

❏ popularized swing music more than anyone else
❏ forced the issue of racial integration in the music business becoming the first bandleader to perform in public with an integrated band
❏ brought jazz out of the bars, clubs, and taverns into the finest concert halls in the world; his band was the first non-classical ensemble to appear at Carnegie Hall

Edward Kennedy "Duke" Ellington (1899-1974) piano / bandleader / composer / arranger

"All musicians should get together on one certain day and get down on their knees to thank Duke."

—Miles Davis, jazz musician

❏ born in Washington D.C.; his mother and father ran the household of a prominent Washington D.C. physician, Dr. M.F. Cuthbert, who attended the families of congressmen and other notables
❏ learned to play the piano by running piano rolls through a player piano's mechanism at a slow speed and following the activated keys with his fingers

"I was raised in the palm of the hand. I was pampered and pampered and spoiled rotten by all the women in the family, aunts and cousins. My parents were very strict; very strict about seeing that I got everything that I wanted."

—Duke Ellington - *Music Is My Mistress*, autobiography

❏ in high school, Ellington had to choose between his music or sports - he was an emerging track star

"After performing at various parties, i learned that when you were playing the piano, there was always a pretty girl standing down at the bass clef end of the piano. I ain't been no athlete since."

—Duke Ellington - *Music Is My Mistress*, autobiography

1922 - first venture into New York failed as he could not find steady work in music

1923 - returned to New York and found success with a small music ensemble performing odd jobs, parties, picnics, etc.

1923-1926 - began writing original compositions and trying to sell them with little success

1926 - caught the attention of **Irving Mills,** who became Duke's agent and manager

1927 - Mills secured the house band job for Ellington at the famous **Cotton Club** in Harlem (a black exploitation club operated by whites for a whites-only audience featuring black musicians, singers, dancer, and comedians in a jungle motif)

- ❏ Ellington became the music director of the **Cotton Club,** responsible for writing the music for the show - music for his band, singers, dancers, and comedy skits
- ❏ the shows were broadcast nationally on weekends making Duke Ellington a rising star in the music business
- ❏ Ellington left the Cotton Club in 1932 and proceeded to become one of the most popular swing artists of the big band era
- ❏ Ellington composed dozens of popular hits during the swing era including:

> - *Satin Doll*
> - *Don't Get Around Much Anymore*
> - *I'm Beginning To See The Light*
> - *Do Nothing Till You Hear From Me*
> - *Perdido*
> - *I've Got It Bad and That Ain't Good*
> - *In A Sentimental Mood*
> - *Solitude*
> - *Mood Indigo*
> - *Sophisticated Lady*

- ❏ jazz author Mark Gridley discusses the seven "books" that comprise Ellington's musical repertoire (from *Jazz Styles*, pp.121-122)

> 1. impressionistic book, or **tone poems**; pieces that describe places, moods, people, culture, etc.
> 2. romantic ballads
> 3. exotic book
> 4. concert book
> 5. concertos
> 6. sacred concerts
> 7. popular song book

- ❏ Ellington's **concertos** are unique in jazz; a **concerto** is performed by a soloist with large ensemble accompaniment (all of the great European master composers, Beethoven, Mozart, etc. composed concertos for soloist and orchestra)

Ellington's Tone Poems
(or impressionistic book)

A tone poem is a composition in which an idea, place, person, event, etc. serves as a basis for the piece; Ellington, through his many tone poems, brought urban black culture to middle-class America.

Duke Ellington's Legacy to Jazz

- ❏ more than any other artist of his time, Ellington brought the essence of black urban culture through his music to middle-class America
- ❏ his compositions were complex and borrowed from classical music forms such as the concerto and suite
- ❏ Ellington brought a sense of dignity and "class" to jazz; he was responsible for raising the perception of jazz music in the eyes of music critics and historians
- ❏ his writing techniques took off where Fletcher Henderson left off in terms of sound

textures, creating moods, and introducing new cross-section voicing techniques (e.g. scoring a chord between the saxes and the trombones instead of just the saxes or just the trombones)

❑ he became the most decorated and honored jazz musician in American history:

- Presidential Medal of Freedom (highest civilian award in the U.S.)
- French Legion of Honor
- Honorary Doctorate Degrees from Yale University, Columbia University, Brown University, St. John's University, University of Wisconsin, and Berklee School of Music in Boston
- served on the National Council for the Arts
- served as a director for the American Academy of Arts and Sciences
- member of the Songwriter's Hall Of Fame

William "Count" Basie (1904-1984) - piano / bandleader

❑ Count Basie's music was representative of the **Kansas City** big band style:

- blues-based music
- improvisation remained the primary focus, not secondary to the arrangement - arrangements were not written down
- each musician in the band "stored" his musical part in his head; the band became well-known for its **"head arrangements"**
- compositions were mostly repeated **riffs**, or **riff tunes** (easy to remember)
- music was not glossed over; it was rough around the edges, but honest and passionate

❑ Basie's rhythm section, **The All-American Rhythm Section**, was a hard-driving unit and a favorite with dancers because of the solid beat that they produced

❑ ironically, Basie was originally from Red Bank, New Jersey, and he played in nightclubs in Harlem as a young musician

❑ Basie studied for a time with **Fats Waller** (himself a former student of **James P. Johnson)**

❑ Basie ended up in Kansas City by accident; he was stranded there in 1928 after a vaudeville tour (for which he was the pianist) folded

❑ Basie's formal music training stood out in a town that had very little formal culture and he soon became the most "in-demand" pianist in Kansas City

❑ the funky approach that he picked up from his teacher, Fats Waller, blended perfectly with the blues-based jazz bands in Kansas City; by 1934, Basie had his own band

❑ Basie often played only a few notes during his piano solos; he could literally make one note swing hard by the way he perfectly placed it within the beat

❑ Basie's style of piano playing used space to create musical tension where most everyone else used space to relieve musical tension

❑ in a word, his piano playing could be described as **"economical"**

Two Tenor Saxophonists:
Coleman Hawkins and Lester Young

	C. Hawkins	L. Young
tone quality	warm, deep tone; full-bodied sound	cool, buoyant tone; light sound
improvisation style	harmonic-based; non-lyrical, angular lines	melodic-based; lyrical, scale-wise lines
improvisatory character	intense, outgoing; somewhat abstract	outgoing, but relaxed; K.C. blues influences
swing feel	swinging, on-top-of the beat; pushing the tempo	swinging, laid-back feel
solo density	complex, lots of notes; little use of space	bursts of notes followed by space
rate of vibrato	medium to fast	little use of vibrato
discovered by	Fletcher Henderson	Count Basie
influenced	Johnny Hodges Charlie Parker Sonny Rollins John Coltrane Michael Brecker	Charlie Parker Woody Herman Stan Getz Paul Desmond David Sanborn

Coleman Hawkins (1904-1969) - tenor sax "Father of the Tenor Sax"

❑ considered the *first important saxophone soloist in jazz*; rose to fame with Fletcher Henderson's Band in the 1920's
❑ considered to be the first significant tenor saxophone soloist in jazz
❑ set down the standards for a specific style of saxophone playing that greatly influenced many of those who followed:

- warm, deep tone with a full-bodied sound
- extensive use of **vibrato**
- aggressive, dense improvisations (lots of notes)
- angular, harmonic-based improvised lines; non-lyrical approach
- intense rhythmic feel: on-top-of the beat (the opposite of laid-back)
- bluesy quality

❑ performed with his own band during the swing era years

Lester Young (1909-1959) - tenor sax
"Prez" (President of the Tenor Sax)

❑ along with Coleman Hawkins, one of the most influential tenor saxophonists in jazz
❑ provided a clear alternative approach to playing the tenor sax:

27

- cool, buoyant tone with a lighter sound
- very little use of vibrato
- bursts of notes followed by space
- smooth, scale-based improvised lines; lyrical approach
- relaxed, laid-back Kansas City swing feel
- coming from Kansas City, his playing was more blues-based and much more relaxed than Coleman Hawkins

❏ rose to fame with, and performed throughout the swing era in Count Basie's Band

Eleanora Fagan Gough (1915-1959) - vocalist

Gough's complex, tragic life, laced with drug addiction, was reflected in her emotional, bluesy vocal style which greatly influenced jazz and popular artists who followed in her footsteps.

❏ born in Baltimore, raised by relatives and was a prostitute call girl by age 10.
❏ music was her emotional release; she loved Bessie Smith and learned all of her songs by listening to recordings

1927 - moved to New York; continued in prostitution

1930 - auditioned for a position as a singing cocktail waitress in a Harlem club and won the job; this was her escape from the world of prostitution; changed her name to **BILLIE HOLIDAY** - in honor of her favorite movie actress, Billie Day

1935 - John Hammond became her representative and she made her first recordings

❏ Holiday's vocal style was blues-based, even though she rarely sang blues songs:

- **melodic paraphrasing:** varied the melody without losing sight of it
- **blues note substitutions:** she would often bend a note to give it a bluesy, or melancholy sound
- **melismatic phrasing:** a rhythmic approach involving holding a note longer than the original version and catching up by singing the succeeding notes faster than the original (or leaving them out altogether)
- Holiday rarely used scat singing techniques

❏ 1937 - toured briefly with Count Basie; met Lester Young; Young and Holiday became very close lifelong friends; Young appeared on many of her recordings

Ella Fitzgerald (1918-1996) - vocalist

❏ born in Yonkers, New York, Ella first gained recognition in 1934 as a 16 year-old amateur-night winner at the famed Apollo Theater in Harlem
❏ immediately hired by bandleader **Chick Webb**; made her first recordings and had a million-selling hit record, *A Tisket A Tasket,* in 1938
❏ Fitzgerald was a study in contrasting style to the melancholy, blues-based Billie Holiday
❏ Fitzgerald perfected the art of **scat singing** and she often took her own scat improvisation alongside the other horn soloists in the band

- ❏ unlike other scat singers who utilized nonsense syllables, Ella often used the actual lyrics to the song while she scatted, or improvised melodic lines
- ❏ she was a **master of improvisation;** on the same level as the best horn players in jazz; her improvisations were outgoing, and upbeat
- ❏ she had a distinctive, immediately recognizable voice:

  - ■ tremendous vocal range: extremely low to ultra high
  - ■ bright, pure, buoyant sound with a shade of "grit" around the edges
  - ■ clean, controlled use of vibrato, but not to the extreme
  - ■ sang every pitch perfectly, although she employed scoops, smears and slides for effect

- ❏ while she recorded many blues songs, Ella's style was not blues-based; on the other hand, Billie Holiday, whose style was bluesy, made relatively few recordings of blues songs
- ❏ However, like Holiday, Fitzgerald utilized melismatic phrasing techniques as well as melodic paraphrasing.

Primary Reasons for the Demise of the Swing Era After 1945

- ■ economics (rising costs in providing steady work for swing bands)
- ■ Musicians Union recording ban (1942-1943)
- ■ rise in popularity of vocalists (Frank Sinatra, etc.)
- ■ emergence of rhythm & blues and country music into mainstream pop

7. Modern Jazz - Bebop

Pages 133-165

After 1945, jazz splintered into three primary camps:

- **jump bands** - swing meets rhythm & blues (one of the primary roots of rock and roll); very danceable & accessible to popular audiences
- **bebop** - jazz developed by and for virtuoso musicians; attracted performers with outgoing musical personalities; small, dedicated audiences
- **cool** - jazz for the intellectual; formal compositions combined with reflective improvisations; at first, very little audience appeal; gradual exposure in motion picture and television soundtracks greatly increased audiences

Jump Bands

❑ cut-down instrumentation of the swing band:

- 1 or 2 trumpets
- 1 trombone (sometimes omitted)
- 3 saxophones (alto, tenor, baritone)
- piano
- bass
- guitar (and/or vibes)
- drums

❑ rhythm and blues repertoire; extensive use of riff-based tunes
❑ hard-driving rhythm section; loud drumming patterns with strong dance beats (the forerunner to early rock and roll)
❑ focus on showmanship and audience involvement, especially dancing
❑ outgoing, blues-based improvisations; extensive use of riffs by soloists in building their improvisations; lots of high register shrieks and wails
❑ two dynamic levels: loud and louder

Bebop

It is not clear why the term "bebop" was used to describe the new jazz style that emerged out of the swing era:

- scat singing syllables, usually used at the end of a scat phrase
- the name of an early bebop recording made by Dizzy Gillespie

❑ developed in the "after-hours" clubs in Harlem and other New York nightspots:

- Minton's
- Monroe's Uptown House

❏ grew out of the cutting contests between musicians held after working hours (after the dance halls and ballrooms closed)
❏ stressed virtuosic technique, long, complicated solo improvisations, and an intentional move away from the constrictions of playing swing music
❏ developed a cult identity:

- zoot suits
- goatees
- sunglasses (shades)
- string ties
- berets, or tams
- slang
- political overtones (modern, ultra-liberal philosophies)

A Comparison of Jazz Styles 1900-1948

	Early Jazz	**Swing**	**Bebop**
group size	combo: 5-8 players	band: 12-15 players	combo: 3-6 players
primary focus	collective and solo improvisation	written compositions and arrangements combined with solo improvisation	solo improvisations; "jam session" approach; spontaneous performances
solos	short in length; melodic paraphrasing with references to ragtime phrasing	short to long lengths with extensive use of riff-based ideas to build solo lines	long solos; dense and syncopated lines, virtuosic in nature
repertoire	ragtime pieces, marches, popular songs	popular songs, show tunes; a few original compositions	original melodies composed over existing song structures
popularity	regional, then national popularity	mainstream popular music between 1935-1945	small, dedicated audiences
rhythmic feel	ragtime phrasing; transition to swing; march beat patterns	swinging, dance beats; foot-tapping rhythms	syncopated, elusive beat patterns; difficult rhythmic ideas
primary lead instr.	cornet/trumpet	trumpet / sax	sax / trumpet
notable soloists	Louis Armstrong Bix Beiderbecke Sidney Bechet Earl "Fatha" Hines	Benny Goodman Count Basie Lester Young Coleman Hawkins	Charlie Parker Dizzy Gillespie Thelonius Monk Max Roach
notable composers	Jelly Roll Morton Fats Waller	Duke Ellington Fletcher Henderson	Charlie Parker Dizzy Gillespie

Dizzy Gillespie (1917-1993) - trumpet

❏ first and most influential bebop trumpeter; achieved world-wide fame - more than any other bebop musician
❏ playing characteristics:

- big, full brassy tone
- outgoing musical personality
- preferred high-register playing
- created intense, syncopated, yet very accessible improvised lines

❏ performed in swing bands led by Ella Fitzgerald, Charlie Barnet, Earl "Fatha" Hines, Cab Calloway, and Billy Eckstine
❏ joined forces with alto saxophonist Charlie Parker in 1945 and made the first important bebop recordings after the Musicians Union recording ban

Charlie Parker (1920-1955) - alto sax

❏ born in Kansas City and raised on the Kansas City jazz scene; idolized Lester Young
❏ as a teenager, he transcribed and learned to play all of Lester Young's recorded solos with Count Basie
❏ encouraged by Young to go to New York; arrived there in 1939

1939: dishwasher at Jimmy's Chicken Shack; nicknamed "Bird"; heard pianist Art Tatum; transferred Tatum's piano licks to the alto sax

1939 - 1942: worked in several "taxi" dance bands

1940 - 1942: steady work with Jay McShann Band; attended jam sessions at Minton's and other after-hours clubs

1942 - 1944: worked with Earl Hines Band along with Dizzy Gillespie

1944 - 1945: worked with Billy Eckstine's Band; considered the first bebop big band; few recordings exist because of the Musicians Union recording ban

1945 - 1946: famous quintet (Charlie Parker's Reboppers) with Dizzy Gillespie; first significant bebop recordings

• Took pauses during his solos at odd beats

Parker's Style

❏ influenced greatly by **Lester Young:**

- light, buoyant saxophone sound with little use of vibrato
- use of space in his solos
- laid-back swinging quality, smooth, effortless performances
- use of blues-based riffs
- use of popular song melodic fragments in his solos: also known as **"quoting"**

❏ influenced somewhat by **Coleman Hawkins**

- complex, dense solos
- aggressive solos, angular melodic lines

1946: Los Angeles performances; drug bust; time spent in jail and drug rehabilitation in Camarillo State Hospital near Santa Barbara

1947 - 1948: back to New York; formed new quintet featuring Miles Davis, a young trumpet player from East St. Louis; **Royal Roost Club** radio broadcasts provided Parker with a larger audience, although small in comparison to audiences enjoyed by swing band leaders and musicians

1949 - 1953: inconsistent performances and recordings due to increasing dependency on narcotics and alcohol; excellent recordings with strings (1949); Parker appreciated classical music and listened intently to 20th century symphonic music

1954 - 1955: rare performances due to deteriorating physical condition; a few excellent musical moments

Parker died on March 12, 1955 - before his 35th birthday - the result of ulcers and cirrhosis of the liver. The coroner estimated his age at death as 55. He was watching the Dorsey Brothers television show when he passed away. His death was announced in the obituary section of the Washington Post - three days later.

Charlie Parker's Legacy to Jazz

❑ he brought bebop to maturity
❑ he inspired a legion of followers such as Sonny Stitt, Phil Woods, and others
❑ he defined the mainstream for the saxophone
❑ he brought a new complexity to his playing that "anchors the bop ideal" (David W. Megill, author)
❑ his solo lines were free of the cliché patterns heard in most other soloists
❑ his phrasing transcended bar lines and chord changes
❑ despite his rapid solo lines, he managed to add expressive inflections to even the shortest sounding notes
❑ he remains the model of improvisational greatness into the 21st century

....
"I loved Bird. He was so good to me. He turned me on to Stravinsky, to Bartok, to the dance, to painters. He was a brilliant man. He had an extensive vocabulary; he rarely used slang. He painted for a while; he encouraged me."
- Sheila Jordan, vocalist
....

....
"Bird was the other half of my heartbeat."
—Dizzy Gillespie, trumpeter
....

....
"Bird used to play 40 different styles; he was never content to remain the same. Bird used to make me play, try to play. He used to lead me on the bandstand. I used to quit every night. The tempo was so up, the challenge was so great.
—Miles Davis, trumpeter
....

Dexter Gordon (1923 - 1990) - tenor sax

❑ Gordon was the premier bebop tenor saxophonist during the period of jazz history dominated by Charlie Parker (late 1940's to early 1950's)
❑ unlike Parker, Gordon's career was productive until his death in 1990
❑ in many ways, Gordon's improvisation style was similar to Parker's:

■ long, flowing lines contrasted with short, irregular, syncopated phrases
■ inserted short quotes of popular songs in his solos
■ impressive displays of virtuosic technique contrasted with soulful, bluesy lines

❑ Gordon's saxophone sound was based more on the Coleman Hawkins' model whereas Parker's sound was influenced by Lester Young
❑ like Parker, Gordon was an important influence on succeeding tenor saxophonists providing the bridge between Coleman Hawkins in the 1930's and John Coltrane in the 1950's
❑ in 1986, was nominated for an Academy Award for Best Supporting Actor in the movie, 'Round Midnight (highly recommended movie about jazz culture)

Thelonius Monk (1917-1982) - piano, composer

❑ Thelonius Monk was a unique jazz musician whose solos were unorthodox and not always in the mainstream of bebop.
❑ Monk became a walking symbol of the bebop revolution:

■ wore bebop clothes
■ spoke bebop language
■ considered himself an artist and his music an art form
■ possessed liberal musical philosophies - always playing at, or beyond, the known boundaries of mainstream jazz

❑ Monk was a formidable composer who wrote pieces that were NOT based upon existing popular song forms
❑ his compositions contained abstract melodic lines and unusual harmony

❏ Monk's rhythmic feel was very stark, syncopated, and, at times, non-swinging (when everyone else in the band was swinging hard!)
❏ Monk explored **dissonance** in music

■ notes that purposely clash with other notes
■ notes that cause tension with the established tonality. (e.g. notes that sound "wrong")

❏ In 1957, Monk recorded an album of solo piano interpretations of well-known popular songs; however, the performances were abstract interpretations of these songs - hardly recognizable to the casual ear.

Bud Powell (1924-1966) - piano

❏ Bud Powell was the most imitated bebop pianist; he influenced nearly every succeeding jazz pianist who followed.
❏ Powell de-emphasized the activity in the left hand; he took the "stride" out of jazz piano playing
❏ Powell re-focused the importance of right hand improvised melodic lines in jazz piano playing; his improvisations were at the same level as Charlie Parker
❏ Powell used the left hand sporadically - to occasionally play a chord underneath the improvised activity of the right hand
❏ Powell also perfected the **"locked-hands"** technique whereby both hands played simultaneously in parallel motion with the melody note in the right little finger and complex harmony notes in the other fingers, lower on the keyboard

8. Cool Jazz (and West Coast Style)

	Bebop	**Cool**
improvisatory character	aggressive; outgoing in nature	reflective; softer approach
instrumentation	trumpet, sax, rhythm section (pno., bass, drums)	trumpet, sax, rhythm section; use of orchestral instruments (strings, wood-winds, tuba, French horn, percussion)
written arrangements	no	yes
compositions	generally, new melodies composed over existing popular song structures	newly composed pieces incorporating classical elements, artistic methods and bebop improvisation
use of counterpoint	no; melodies performed in unison by horns	yes; composed counter-point interjected with solo improvisation
use of dynamics	no (loud and louder)	yes; notated in the music
popularity	small, dedicated audience	gradually quite popular due to exposure in film and television soundtracks

❑ cool jazz began as a reaction to the explosive frenzy of bebop; its musicians strove for a more sophisticated, mature style

❑ cool jazz musicians insisted on being considered the equals of classical musicians and therefore borrowed many procedures from classical music

❑ the term "cool jazz" refers to an attitude more than a style of music; however, cool jazz tends to be softer and more academic in nature than bebop

❑ cool jazz improvisations are modeled after bebop, with a more reflective and soft-ened attitude; cool jazz musicians play rapid bebop passages, but contrast them with space and subtle melodic lines

❑ by the 1950's, cool jazz tended to be played more on the west coast by west coast musicians while bebop remained more prominent on the east coast

❑ however, the first significant national recordings in the cool style were made on the east coast by Miles Davis, Gerry Mulligan, Gil Evans and several other impor-tant east coast jazz musicians

Miles Davis (1926-1991): Birth of the Cool

During his tenure with Charlie Parker in New York in the late 1940's, Miles Davis became fascinated with a new approach to bebop performance initiated by a young group of musicians and composers who wanted to combine the essence of bop with structured, complex written arrangements in the tradition of Duke Ellington. This new approach to bebop was led by pianist **Lennie Tristano** and alto saxophonist **Lee Konitz**, whose band featured new compositions and arrangements by its two leaders as well as young writers such as **Gil Evans, John Lewis,** and **Gerry Mulligan.**

After leaving Charlie Parker's quintet in 1948, Miles organized his own band based upon the style of the Tristano/Konitz ensemble. Many of the musicians who were playing with Tristano and Konitz became members of Miles' band as well - including Lee Konitz himself. Arranger Gil Evans, who wrote music for the Claude Thornhill band during the swing era, was a key contributor to the sound of the Miles Davis group scoring unusual, complex arrangements of bebop tunes for trumpet, trombone, alto sax, baritone sax, french horn, tuba, and rhythm (piano, bass, drums). The use of the french horn was a first in modern jazz and the tuba had not been regularly used in jazz performances since the early 1920's. In writing for the ensemble, Evans utilized **cross-section voicing techniques,** introduced and refined by Duke Ellington several years earlier, as well as pioneering the use of **dissonance** (notes that clash, or seem "wrong") in jazz to evoke textural ideas and to "jolt" the audience.

Another primary characteristic of the Davis ensemble was the lighter, buoyant sound of the music: Davis and Evans focused on the use of quieter volume levels **(dynamics),** a missing element in the bebop music of Charlie Parker and others. The quieter nature of the Davis group, combined with the structured musical arrangements, resulted in a clear alternative to the sound of mainstream bebop and led to several performances by the band at the Royal Roost Club in New York. Between January, 1949 and March, 1950 the Miles Davis Nonet made three recording sessions for Capitol Records featuring compositions by Gil Evans, Gerry Mulligan, and John Lewis. Although the Nonet failed to perform outside of New york and had disbanded by the time their recordings were released, they introduced what would soon be called "cool jazz" to the world. By the time Capitol reissued these landmark recordings in the mid-1950's, the term "cool jazz" was a cliche in music: nevertheless, Capitol renamed the album *The Birth of the Cool* because, in an historical sense, it was.

Dave Brubeck (1920-   ) - piano

Brubeck came to prominence in San Francisco during the 1950's and has remained one of the most popular jazz artists into the 1990's. Three years before the Miles Davis *Birth of the Cool* sessions, Brubeck was making similar recordings as a student of composer Darious Milhaud, who encouraged the use of jazz elements in formal 20th century composition. Next to Miles Davis, Brubeck became the most popular jazz artist during the 1960's, performing sold-out concerts around the world and making recordings that consistently sold 100,000 copies, or more.

Modern Jazz Quartet
featuring
John Lewis (1920-   ) - piano / composer
Milt Jackson (1923-   ) - vibraphone (vibes)

❏ one of the most significant jazz quartets of all-time, the MJQ projected the image a classical string quartet:

- ■ wore tuxedos in performances
- ■ performed in the finest music halls
- ■ provided audiences with printed programs and program notes
- ■ performed well-rehearsed music with the ensemble tightness of the finest string quartets
- ■ featured new, complex compositions written by John Lewis

❏ the MJQ introduced the concept of **Third Stream Jazz** - a term coined by jazz author and orchestra conductor **Gunther Schuller** in describing their music:

- ■ 1st Stream: jazz music
- ■ 2nd Stream : classical music
- ■ **3rd Stream:** classical music and jazz music combined (half-way between jazz and classical)

(One of the first attempts by a well-known classical composer to write a piece for a jazz ensemble was Igor Stravinsky's *Ebony Concerto* for Woody Herman's Band in 1945.)

❏ John Lewis composed many pieces for the MJQ and classical instruments combining jazz improvisation with classical-style composition

❏ in Lewis's compositions, the classical musicians were never assigned the task of playing in a jazz style, just as the MJQ were never required to play classical elements; this ensured that jazz and classical were being performed simultaneously without compromise to either style

Stan Getz (1927 - 1991) - tenor sax

❏ while Getz thought of himself as a bebopper, his sound and style were considered by critics and listeners as cool; part of this had to do with his "cool" image and personality

❏ Getz took the lighter, buoyant sound of Lester Young to a further level in producing a more airy, feathered sound; his nickname was "The Sound"

❏ musically, Getz was an aggressive player and to many listeners, his style could be considered bebop

❏ Getz was also influenced by pre-20th century classical music; his improvisations were once described as "classical melodies"

❏ during the 1960's, Getz became commercially popular when he recorded bossa nova music from Brazil and scored a top 40 hit record with vocalist Astrud Gilberto, *The Girl From Ipanema*

❏ his long, influential career continued until his death in 1991

9. Bebop to Hard Bop - East Coast Style

After Charlie Parker's death in 1955, bebop took on new musical characteristics that enabled the style to re-emerge and challenge the popularity of cool jazz. While maintaining its roots in the classic bebop playing of Charlie Parker, a crop of younger musicians brought new life into the style, making the music more accessible to a larger audience without compromising its integrity. The transition from classic bebop to hard bop was seamless and many of the older beboppers became identified with the new movement. In contrast to the cool jazz style which was identified with west coast musicians, hard bop became identified with the east coast jazz scene.

Hard Bop (or East Coast Style)
Comparison of Bebop and Hard Bop

	Bebop	**Hard Bop**
improvisations	outgoing, aggressive, complex, angular in nature	outgoing, aggressive, bluesy qualities; tendency towards lyricism
blues elements	blues form for improvisation; few references to bluesy ideas; abstract blues variations; strong elements of Rhythm & Blues; gospel	blues form for improvisation; lots of blues-style riffs, licks, and feeling
written arrangements	no	yes
compositions	new, bebop melodic lines composed over existing pop tune structures	new compositions not necessarily based upon previous pop tune structures
use of counterpoint	no; unison playing	yes; counter-melodies used
rhythmic feel	syncopated; abstract drum patterns, difficult for the average listener to follow	hard-edged, swinging drum patterns with a focus on the backbeat; suitable for dancing
instrumentation	combos: 3-5 players (sax, trumpet, piano, bass, drums)	combos: 3-5 players (sax, trumpet, piano, bass, drums)
important soloists	Charlie Parker (alto sax) Dizzy Gillespie (trumpet) Bud Powell (piano) Thelonius Monk (piano) Max Roach (drums)	Cannonball Adderley (a.sax) Sonny Rollins (tenor sax) Horace Silver (piano) Wes Montgomery (guitar) Art Blakey (drums)

Sonny Rollins (1929-   ) - tenor sax

Rollins is considered a transitional figure in jazz, and one of the most gifted improvisers in history. He made his first important impact as a member of Miles Davis's group in the early 1950's. His aggressive bebop approach contrasted nicely with Miles' cool jazz style which contributed to the success of the band and its acceptance by a larger jazz audience of both bebop and cool listeners.

Horace Silver (1928-   ) - piano / composer

❏ Silver represents the essence of the hard bop style:

- strong elements of rhythm & blues & gospel in his playing; **funky style**
- use of simple, riff phrases in building melodic lines; lyrical approach
- use of silence as a dramatic device
- his compositions utilized some of the jump band ideas practiced by Lionel Hampton, etc. (background horn riffs, bluesy shout choruses, etc.)

❏ in addition to his skills as a pianist, Silver is one of the most prolific composers in jazz with dozens of his tunes included in the standard repertoire of jazz musicians (*Sister Sadie, Song For My Father, The Preacher, Doodlin'*, etc.)

Julian "Cannonball" Adderley (1928-1975) - alto sax

❏ considered by many to be the best alto saxophonist after Charlie Parker, Adderley made his first important recordings with Miles Davis between 1956-1959
❏ Adderley's stylistic traits represent the essence of hard bop:

- big, full tone on the alto sax; sometimes mistaken, even by other musicians, as a tenor sax
- funky, blues-laced solos; this set him apart from Parker
- virtuosic technique; often played bursts of notes followed by sparse, lyrical lines
- aggressive, outgoing improvisatory character

Wes Montgomery (1925-1968) - guitar

The 1960's was the "decade of the guitar" as rock music and rock guitarists dominated American popular music. Wes Montgomery brought the guitar into focus in jazz during the 1960's becoming one of that decade's most influential jazz musicians. Along with Jimi Hendrix and Eric Clapton, Wes Montgomery was considered the best of the 1960's-era guitar virtuosos. Montgomery's style was "hard-core" hard bop:

- funky, bluesy improvisations, laced with rhythm & blues elements
- aggressive, outgoing improvisational character
- long, flowing, virtuosic **horn-like lines** (remember Earl Hines?)
- use of **octave voicings** to reinforce his melodic lines (remember Earl Hines?)
- unlike Hendrix or Clapton, Montgomery's electric guitar sound was clean and pure, without amplified distortion; however, his volume was louder than previous electric guitarists (and more aggressive in nature)

Montgomery was one of the first jazz musicians to record an album featuring songs by The Beatles (*A Day In The Life*, 1967, A & M Records). Montgomery's sudden death in

1968 (heart attack) happened at a time when his albums were selling in the hundreds of thousands and his concerts were always sold-out.

10. Miles Davis (1926-1991) - trumpet

Miles Davis changed the sound of jazz several times during his career of nearly 50 years; he either led the way himself, or inspired others to strike out on a different path.

❏ grew up in East St. Louis, Illinois; father was a dental surgeon and a big band enthusiast; his mother wanted him to learn to play the violin; his father insisted upon the trumpet
❏ studied trumpet with Elwood Buchanon, a symphonic musician in St. Louis; Buchanon preferred a subtle, less brassy trumpet tone and discouraged the use of a vibrato - two factors which would characterize Miles' style throughout his career

Miles Davis Trumpet Style

❏ soft, hollow, plaintive trumpet tone; avoidance of brassy sound
❏ complete avoidance of vibrato; prefers a straight, unwavering tone
❏ extensive use of the Harmon mute (produces a buzzing, thin metallic sound)
❏ preference for the low to middle range of the trumpet
❏ use of high notes restricted to a few, selected occurrences

Miles Davis Improvisatory Tendencies

❏ melodic lines skillfully constructed; usually theme & variation approach
❏ dramatic devices utilized such as:

■ holding single notes longer than expected (melismatic phrasing) emphasizing dissonant notes
■ using intricate syncopated rhythms
■ extensive use of space

❏ avoidance of jazz clichés, or standard "licks"; his improvisations always contained new and fresh-sounding ideas
❏ master of self-restraint; played only what was necessary to get his musical idea across
❏ reflective, cool nature in his playing
❏ projected a "cool" attitude as well (in his choice of cars, clothes, speaking manner, etc.)
❏ appropriate use of vocalistic effects, although understated (scoops, smears, rips, etc. used sparingly)
❏ used his virtuosic technique sparingly; rarely played long, dense melodies

❏ chose a more lyrical approach, although he would construct angular, abstract melodic lines if the situation called for it

1944: first break; substitute trumpet player in Billy Eckstine's Band in St. Louis (Musicians Union call); met Dizzy Gillespie and Charlie Parker, featured soloists in the band.

1944: accepted into the Julliard School of Music (New York) classical music program; dismissed from the school a short time later for practicing jazz in the school's practice rooms (Miles insisted that he left on his own)

1944-1947: multitude of playing opportunities with various jazz musicians in New York

1947-48: member of Charlie Parker's band

1948-49: development of new music culminating in the Birth of the Cool sessions in 1949; the emergence of a new jazz style led by Miles himself

1950-53: various recordings and performances under his own name; problems with drug dependency limited his success

1953-55: decision to stop using narcotics resulted in his first successful band with Sonny Rollins and several important recordings

1955-56: breakthrough years, artistically and commercially; one of the most famous quintets in history now known as the **Miles Davis Classic Quintet**

- ■ Miles Davis - trumpet
- ■ John Coltrane - tenor sax
- ■ Red Garland - piano
- ■ Paul Chambers - bass
- ■ Philly Joe Jones - drums

❏ the Miles Davis Classic Quintet is considered to be one of the most successful jazz ensembles in history

■ commercial success

• sold hundreds of thousands of recordings
• played sold-out concerts all over the world

■ artistic success

• the essence of 1950's jazz; the model of greatness from that period
• featured the two most influential improvisors after Charlie Parker (Davis and Coltrane)

Gil Evans (1912-1988)

1957: Miles Davis and arranger Gil Evans teamed-up to record the music of **Porgy And Bess,** an opera composed in the 1930's by **George Gershwin;** Davis and Evans had worked together in the late 1940's on the *Birth of The Cool* sessions;

- *Porgy And Bess*, featured Davis improvising over lush, complex arrangements by Evans
- scored for standard big band and other woodwind and brass instruments including flutes, French horns and tuba
- Davis's Porgy And Bess recording can be considered **Third Stream jazz**

1960: another David/Evans Third Stream recording, **Sketches Of Spain**, brought together Spanish classical music and jazz improvisation:

- Evans scored the background accompaniment parts for brass, woodwinds, and percussion - not the traditional jazz big band.
- *Sketches Of Spain* came about after Miles heard a recording of *Concierto de Aranjuez for Guitar & Orchestra* by Spanish composer Joaquin Rodrigo

....

"I couldn't get it out of my mind. Then when Gil and I decided to do another album, I played him the record and he liked it. As we usually do, we planned the program first by ourselves for about two months. I work out something; he takes it home and works on it some more: and then we figure out how we're going to do it. He can read my mind and I can read his."

—Miles Davis; *Sketches Of Spain* liner notes

....

Modal Jazz - "Kind Of Blue"

Prior to the development of modern scales and harmonies culminating in the music of J.S. Bach in the 18th century Baroque period, European music was based upon **modes.** Instead of a complex system of moving chords and changing key centers (scales), Medieval music was based upon a single key center, or mode. The basic modes included the Dorian, Phrygian, Lydian and Mixo-lydian; eventually, these modes evolved into the modern major and minor scales. Miles Davis was the first significant jazz musician to experiment successfully with jazz improvisation based upon Medieval modes:

- single key center allowed more freedom for improvisation; not bound by rapid harmony and key center changes
- opened up new horizons for jazz melodic development

. Miles Davis plays on the Dorian mode

The breakthrough recording of modal jazz was made by Miles Davis in 1959 entitled **Kind Of Blue.**

Miles Davis 1960's Quintet

By 1964, Miles assembled another legendary quintet featuring several musicians who would go on to become important leaders on their respective instruments:

❏ **Wayne Shorter - tenor sax / composer**

- aggressive, full-tone sound; a logical replacement for John Coltrane
- Shorter was a first-rate, innovative composer who wrote most of the group's material during his tenure in the band
- most of his compositions have become part of the standard repertoire for jazz musicians

❑ **Herbie Hancock - piano**

- a combination of Horace Silver's gospel approach and Bill Evans' academic, harmonically complex style
- Hancock was the perfect accompanist for Davis and Shorter as well as a unique improviser in his own right

❑ **Ron Carter - bass**

- provided the solid rhythmic underpinning that allowed the creative ideas of the rest of the band to evolve around him
- has recorded over 1,200 jazz albums (with various artists) during his career

❑ **Tony Williams - drums**

- the most innovative drummer during the 1960's, Williams revolutionized jazz (and rock) drumming by:

  - incorporating complex, **layered polyrhythmic patterns** between his hands and feet
  - actively interacting with Davis and Shorter, rhythmically and texturally

- Williams was still a teenager when he joined Davis's band; his energy drove Miles to new heights in creativity

The 1960's Miles Davis Quintet combined traditional cool and hard bop styles with modal and free jazz elements.

Miles Davis and Fusion Jazz

After 1968, Miles Davis moved further away from traditional cool/bebop performances and into music that melded, or fused, rock elements with free and modal jazz styles. While Davis was not the first jazz musician to move in this direction, his two 1969 albums, In *A Silent Way* and *Bitches Brew* established the direction of jazz/rock, or fusion, and inspired many young musicians to strike out on that musical path.

Summary of Important Contributions to Jazz by Miles Davis

❑ Changed the sound of jazz several times during his career of nearly 50 years; he either led the way himself, or inspired others to strike out on a different path:

> 1944-1949 - bebop
> 1949-1991 - cool jazz
> 1959-1991 - modal jazz
> 1964-1991 - free / modal jazz
> 1969-1991 - fusion
> 1980-1991 - techno jazz
> 1990-1991 - hip-hop jazz

❑ Created an original, substantial, and highly influential trumpet style, evident in his first recordings with Charlie Parker as well as his last recordings of hip-hop jazz in the early 1990's.

❑ Produced a large body of distinctive, high-quality recordings which served as a model for contemporary musicians in the way that recordings of Louis Armstrong, Lester Young, and Charlie Parker had served his predecessors.

❑ Introduced many important future jazz greats in his bands throughout his career including:

piano: John Lewis, Red Garland, Bill Evans, Wynton Kelly, Herbie Hancock, Chick Corea, Marcus Miller (synthesizer)

saxophone: Sonny Rollins, Gerry Mulligan, John Coltrane, Cannonball Adderley, Wayne Shorter, Sam Rivers, Benny Maupin

bass: Paul Chambers, Ron Carter, Dave Holland

drums: Max Roach, Kenny Clarke, Art Blakey, Philly Joe Jones, Jimmy Cobb, Tony Williams, Al Foster

guitar: John McLaughlin, George Benson, Larry Coryell, John Scofield

....

"That's what I tell all my musicians; I tell them to be ready to play what you know and play above what you know. Anything might happen above what you've been used to playing."

"When I hear jazz musicians today playing all those same licks we used to play so long ago, I feel sad for them. Most people my age like old, stuffy furniture. I like the new Memphis style of sleek high tech stuff, a lot of it coming from Italy. Bold colors and long, sleek, spare lines. I don't like a lot of clutter."

"I love challenges and new things; they re-energize me. But music has always been healing for me - and spiritual. I'm still learning every day."
                                —Miles Davis, age 65, 1991 (a few months before his death)
....

11. John Coltrane (1926-1967) - tenor/soprano sax

....
"The genius of John Coltrane lies in his technique, his philosophical approach to music, and his intensity. No one was more serious about his music."

—Lewis Porter, jazz historian
....

....
"Music and life are all about style. To Coltrane, music was something more: playing was his research, his intellectual challenge, his means of investigating, as well as expressing spiritual moods."

—Miles Davis, jazz musician
....

❏ Born in Hamlet, North Carolina; moved to Philadelphia with his mother after his father died in 1943.

❏ Studied alto saxophone and music theory at the Ornstein School of Music with tenor saxophonist Benny Golson; drafted into the Navy in 1945; discharged in 1946.

1948: switched to tenor sax playing with Eddie "Cleanhead" Vinson's band; performed with

> 1949 - 1952: Dizzy Gillespie

> 1952 - 1953: Earl Bostic (jump band / rhythm & blues style)

> 1954 - 1955: Johnny Hodges band

....
"We played honest music in that band (Hodges). It was my education into the older generation. I really enjoyed that job. I liked every tune in the book; nothing was superficial. It all had meaning and it swung."

—John Coltrane, from *Coltrane On Coltrane*
....

1955: Miles Davis hired Coltrane on the recommendation of drummer Philly Joe Jones, who was already performing in Miles' band

1955-1956: Miles Davis Classic Quintet brought worldwide recognition to Coltrane; his hard-bop, rhythm & blues style contrasted nicely with Davis's restrained cool style

April, 1957: Davis fired Coltrane after an argument about Coltrane's drug use and unreliability erupted into a backstage fist fight

> ■ shocked by his dismissal, Coltrane returned to Philadelphia and confronted his drug problems by going "cold turkey" at his mother's house:

"During the year 1957, I experienced, by the grace of God, a spiritual awakening which was to lead me to a richer, fuller, more productive life. At that time, in gratitude, I humbly asked to be given the means and privilege to make others happy through music. I feel this was granted through His grace."

—John Coltrane, liner notes from the album *A Love Supreme* (1964)

1957: made his first recordings under his own name, and rejoined Miles Davis in 1958; his technique and improvising skills were astonishing and he was ready to step forward and strike out on a new path

"Giant Steps" Harmonic Structure

B**	D7**	G	Bb7**	Eb		Am7**	D7
G	Bb7**	Eb	F#7**	B		Fm7**	Bb7
Eb		Am7**	D7	G		C#m7**	F#7
B		Fm7**	Bb7	Eb		C#m7**	F#7

Modal Jazz Period

Fascinated by the potential of the modal jazz style (with Miles Davis in 1959), Coltrane led the way in its development during the early 1960's.

Coltrane's Influence - The Classic Quartet

After recording *Kind Of Blue* with Miles Davis, Coltrane formed his own band and began exploring modal and free jazz concepts. This band would rival the artistic achievements of the Miles Davis Quintet and Coltrane himself, would surpass Davis as the most influential jazz musician of the 1960's (and beyond). Coltrane's group became known as the **"Classic Quartet"**:

- **Coltrane - tenor and soprano saxophones**
- **McCoy Tyner - piano**
- **Jimmy Garrison - bass**
- **Elvin Jones - drums**

Coltrane's musical personality evolved after 1960:

- he studied extensively from the music theory books published by Nicolas Slonimsky
- he was also influenced by the avant-gard saxophonist John Gilmore
- furthermore, Coltrane's music took on political overtones (*Alabama, Lonely Woman, The Promise*)
- his compositions explored religious themes (*A Love Supreme, Om*)

Stylistically, Coltrane's playing took on the following characteristics:

- **"Sheets Of Sound"** (coined by jazz critic Ira Gitler); he enveloped his listeners in "sheets of sound"; a "wall of notes" cascading down on his audiences

- **The Sweep:** basically, the attempt by Coltrane to encompass a wide range of musical effects centered around the use of sustaining notes in the bass and piano, long, linear drumming patterns, and long sweeping runs that spanned the entire range of the saxophone
- **The Cry:** Coltrane preferred the higher register on the tenor sax: he would often create rising melodic lines that ultimately sounded as if he were squeezing the high notes out of his horn creating a shrieking, or crying effect

John Coltrane and Free Jazz

During the last two years of his career, Coltrane explored free jazz techniques; his music became far-removed from the hard bop style of a few years earlier. He also became interested in the music of other cultures and tried to blend what he heard into his own music. His last quartet featured:

- **Alice Coltrane (his wife) - piano**
- **Jimmy Garrison - bass**
- **Rashied Ali - drums, tabla, percussion**

Coltrane's free jazz recordings made a lasting impression on younger musicians as evidenced by the fact that his playing techniques have been incorporated into mainstream popular styles (listen to the popular mainstream soprano saxophone style of Kenny G. and elements of John Coltrane's techniques are quite evident).

Coltrane's Legacies to Jazz

- ❑ devised a new approach to saxophone playing that was built upon the Hawkins and Young schools of saxophone playing:

  - bluesy, linear (scale) approach of Lester Young
  - aggressive, dense, big-sound approach of Coleman Hawkins

- ❑ in terms of technique, improvisational skills, and an intense dedication to his art, Coltrane influenced jazz musicians more than anyone else, including Miles Davis, during the 1960's (and beyond)
- ❑ popularized modal jazz techniques (after Miles Davis introduced the concepts)
- ❑ was a leader in the rise of free jazz during the turbulent 1960's
- ❑ popularized the soprano saxophone

....
"He kept trying to reach new levels of awareness, of peace, of spirituality. That's why I regard the music he played as spiritual music - John's way of getting closer and closer to the Creator."

—Albert Ayler, jazz musician
....

12. Avant-Gard/Free Jazz Styles

Free jazz is an umbrella term that describes a large number of styles and artists. The term derives from the observation that performances in this genre are often free of traditional melodic, harmonic, and rhythmic practices.

❑ non-traditional musical characteristics of free jazz include:

- textural improvisation, rather than melodic; "aural sound paintings"
- creation of melodic lines that are:
  - abstract
  - angular - large intervallic leaps
  - stress dissonance
  - sometimes based upon short, melodic fragment bursts
  - free of traditional bebop clichés

- extreme manipulation of pitch and tone quality
  - high-register shrieks and wails
  - low gurgles and squawks
  - unusual playing techniques used to create distortion of sound
  - use of electronics to further alter and distort the sound of instruments

- polytonal approach (several key centers played simultaneously)
- traditional harmony abandoned; use of jazz chords avoided
- piano usually omitted (to avoid setting up harmonies and key centers)
- traditional walking bass lines avoided: bassists took on the role as another lead melodic instrument in the band
- avoidance of traditional "swinging" drum patterns in favor of undercurrent of textural activity; direct interaction with horn players
- avoidance of steady tempos, or rhythms (non-rhythmic feeling)
- use of non-western instruments (new sound textures)

❑ traditional jazz characteristics usually retained in free jazz include:

- emphasis on collective improvisation
- solo improvisation also encouraged
- use of background riffs behind soloists
- examples of carefully composed compositions and arrangements
  - sometimes scored in traditional notation
  - short, cued melodic fragments
  - graphic notation employed (use of artistic symbols to denote certain musical values such as dynamics, pitch, rhythmic activity, etc.)

55

- examples of traditional time-keeping roles played by bass and drums (normal walking bass lines and swing patterns)

Charles Mingus (1922-1979) - bass / composer

❑ Charles Mingus, a free-spirited bassist and composer, is difficult to categorize, musically; his music was influenced by a variety of sources:

- Duke Ellington (compositional techniques and textural explorations)
- Charlie Parker (bebop style)
- Claude Debussy & Maurice Ravel (Impressionistic composers)
- gospel music (he played in his church's gospel band)
- rhythm and blues (incorporated blues ideas in his compositions)
- free jazz (Ornette Coleman, John Coltrane, Eric Dolphy)

❑ along with drummer Max Roach, established the long-running Jazz Workshop loft concert series in New York during the early 1950's.

- modeled after successful classical chamber music loft concerts featuring young performers and new composers
- presented jazz in a formal, yet relaxed setting; introduced many new jazz artists and composers (including Mingus who was having trouble getting noticed in New York)

❑ Mingus was known for his wide variety of compositions including pieces for solo bass, jazz trio and string quartet, brass band, jazz band, standard jazz quintet, and full symphony orchestra

Ornette Coleman (1930-   ) - alto sax / composer

Ornette Coleman remains the leading figure in free jazz into the 1990's. His breakthrough recording of the album, *Free Jazz* (1960), established him as an important innovator in the development of the style. Many of Coleman's performances contain traditional jazz elements, especially in the area of composition. Some of his compositions are quite "catchy" and many are performed by other musicians making him one of the only free jazz composers to contribute to the general repertoire of jazz. *Free Jazz* is considered the springboard recording for the free jazz movement of the 1960's, just as the Miles Davis album, *Birth of the Cool,* heralded the cool jazz era and *Kind Of Blue* defined modal jazz.

Cecil Taylor (1929 -   ) - piano / composer

One of the few pianists to play free jazz, Taylor's music has been described as turbulent, violent, and very imaginative. He has composed music for various ensembles using jazz and orchestral instruments. His tone poems, such as *Enter Evening,* are considered among the finest 20th century avant-gard compositions. *Enter Evening,* representing a departure from his "turbulent" playing style, is more graphically demonstrated in the live recordings of his spontaneous compositions such as *Jitney 2.* As a performer, Cecil Taylor is unmatched in terms of turbulent activity, drama, and energy. While he generally sells few recordings, his concerts are always sold-out; watching him play the piano is an event that cannot be captured effectively on disc.

Association for the Advancement of Creative Musicians or A.A.C.M.

A Chicago-based alliance of black free jazz musicians, the A.A.C.M. has been a "clearing-house" of avant-gard music since its formation in the early 1960's. The primary mission of the A.A.C.M. involves organizing and promoting concerts and recordings of its members as well as providing educational training in music performance and the business of music. Chapters of the A.A.C.M. were established in many cities throughout the United States.

The "flagship" group of the A.A.C.M. is the **Art Ensemble of Chicago**. The Art Ensemble of Chicago displays the essence of the musical direction of the A.A.C.M.:

- free jazz improvisatory performances
- focus on collective, textural improvisations
- occasional performance of traditional hard bop style
- embracement of world musical cultures, especially West African instrumental music
- utilization of exotic instruments such as African wooden flutes, log drums, etc.
- traditional African costumes are worn in performances
- often, poetry is recited in the middle of performances
- light-hearted dramatic skits are sometimes performed as part of the music

Keith Jarrett (1945-   ) - piano / composer

Like Charles Mingus, Keith Jarrett is difficult to categorize musically. His influences are derived from many sources including:

- hard bop (McCoy Tyner approach)
- classical music (Mozart, Chopin, etc.)
- Impressionistic music (Ravel, Debussy)
- stride (Art Tatum)
- boogie woogie (Meade Lux Lewis)
- gospel (Horace Silver)
- country and folk music
- 20th century avant-gard (Stockhausen, Cage, etc.)

❑ first heard in the mid-1960's with avant-gard woodwind player Charles Lloyd; later played with Miles Davis in the early 1970's
❑ Jarrett possesses the technique of a finely-trained concert pianist, and he has appeared many times with symphony orchestras performing various classical piano concertos
❑ Jarrett is well-known for his entirely improvised solo piano concerts during the 1970's
❑ he has performed 2+ hours without a pre-planned program and without playing pre-composed pieces
❑ his improvisations run the gamut of musical styles from hard bop to country to classical and avant-gard free jazz
❑ often, his various improvisations are connected into one, hour-long, uninterrupted piece.
❑ he was one of the few pianists who rejected synthesizer technology in the 1970's
❑ in the 1990's, he performed and recorded with a trio performing traditional standard popular songs in new musical settings.

13. Jazz / Rock or Fusion

The merging of jazz and rock music was inevitable: both musics share similar musical roots (especially the blues), feature improvisation, convey a sense of exhilarating freedom that sets both styles apart from other popular music, and battled the music establishment for respectability.

A Comparison of Rock Music and Jazz / Rock (Fusion)

	Rock	Jazz / Rock
performance type	largely vocal, dance music	largely instrumental, concert music
improvisations	usually short, improvised guitar or keyboard instrumental breaks in between vocal choruses; traditional melodic-based lines	long, instrumental solos based upon electronic textural improvisations and/or virtuosic bebop lines
harmonies	blues-based and/or modal harmony; usually simple chord voicings	complex Impressionistic harmonies and/or modal chord voicings; also, in certain styles, traditional harmonic practices avoided
rhythmic feel	dance beat patterns; focus on strong beats with some syncopation; heavy back-beat	complex variations on rock drumming patterns with added Afro-Cuban, or Latin percussion
bass lines	strong, counter lines that serve as a bottom anchor to the sound of the music; usually repeated riff patterns	syncopated, non-walking lines with melodic interactions with the horn players; use of riff patterns usually avoided
use of electronics	to increase the volume of the music as well as creating distortion in the sound of the music	to increase the intensity of the sound textures through distortion and other non-traditional musical tones
popularity	after 1955, the mainstream of popular music in the U.S.	first jazz style after Swing to gain a popular audience; some recordings reached the top 40 in record sales

Throughout the first ten years of the rock era (1955-1965), jazz musicians distanced themselves from rock music, citing its inferior characteristics (simple chords, lack of high musicianship, commercialism, etc.) and lack of artistic intentions. However, jazz elements had been a part of rock and roll and soul music from the very beginning:

- saxophone improvisations occurred regularly in the recordings of Little Richard and Fats Domino
- early rock and roll drumming patterns were derived from jazz swing beats
- soul bands led by Ray Charles and James Brown featured horn sections who played background riffs that were derived from the big band tradition

By 1966, a group of younger musicians who grew up listening to rock and roll, but discovered jazz through the recordings of Miles Davis, Dave Brubeck, and John Coltrane, emerged with a new attitude about rock music and jazz improvisation.

Gary Burton (1943 -   ) - vibraphone
and
Larry Coryell (1943 -   ) - guitar

Gary Burton was playing jazz with Stan Getz by the time he was 21 years old; at the same time, Larry Coryell was playing rock and roll in Seattle with The Dynamics.

- **Burton:** a young jazz musician who wanted to play music influenced by rock
- **Coryell:** a young rock musician who wanted to play music influenced by jazz

Burton and Coryell met in New York in early 1967, discovered their personal musical goals, and formed a new quartet that would cause a sensation among jazz and rock musicians alike. Burton fused his strong jazz background and improvisational abilities with Coryell's rock approach and distorted guitar sound resulting in the first important jazz/rock recordings made by a known jazz artist (Burton). The recordings made by Coryell and Burton laid the groundwork for the rise in popularity of fusion a few years later. Ironically, both musicians moved away from fusion during the 1970's, preferring to play mainstream jazz styles by the 1980's.

The Rise in Popularity of Jazz / Rock

Before fusion, the term jazz/rock was used to describe the merging of the two musical styles. The first widespread popularity of jazz/rock was achieved by rock bands who employed jazz horn players to augment the sound of their music. The two most popular jazz/rock bands were **Chicago Transit Authority** (later shortened to Chicago), and **Blood, Sweat and Tears.** Both bands featured excellent jazz horn players and recorded jazz-influenced rock tunes that enjoyed success on Billboard's Top 100 including Blood, Sweat & Tears' *Spinning Wheel* (#2, 5/69), and Chicago's *Make Me Smile* (#9, 4/70)

The Breakthrough of Fusion - Miles Davis

By 1969, Miles Davis was moving towards rock-based jazz improvisation; several cuts on albums recorded after 1966 featured **Tony Williams** playing modified rock drumming patterns such as *Freedom Jazz Dance* on *Miles Smiles*. His 1969 album, *In A Silent Way* featured rock-based compositions by keyboardist **Joe Zawinul** and forecasted Davis's landmark **Bitches Brew** album in 1970. Prior to recording **Bitches Brew**, Miles Davis was interviewed in *Rolling Stone Magazine* where he announced his plans to record with established rock musicians. His goal was to merge the energy of funk music (Sly & the Family Stone, George Clinton, etc.) with free form jazz improvisation. The resulting album, **Bitches Brew,** was hailed by young musicians and critics as the beginning of a new era in jazz; the official marriage of rock and jazz styles. Some critics called **Bitches Brew** the "*Sgt. Pepper of jazz,*" referring to the famous Beatles album of 1967. On the other hand, mainstream jazz musicians and critics accused Miles of commercializing his art and severely criticized him in the press; the battle lines were drawn between mainstream jazz and fusion and they remained so twenty years later.

❑ the term fusion emerged as an umbrella term describing any music that contained jazz and rock elements - the fusing of two diverse styles.
❑ stylistic characteristics of **Bitches Brew** included:

■ **modal and/or free jazz improvisations** accompanied by electronic textures and rock/funk drumming patterns
■ elements of **collective, textural improvisation** along with featured solos
■ use of **amplified and/or distorted sound textures** (Miles amplified his trumpet)
■ use of **distorted electric guitar**
■ use of **electric bass** - rarely heard in jazz until this album was made
■ double rhythm section (2 of each instrument); created profound musical interactions:

• 1 jazz, and 1 rock keyboard player
• 1 electric bassist (rock), and 1 acoustic bassist (jazz)
• 1 rock, and 1 jazz drummer

■ use of **exotic percussion instruments**; African drums, shakers, gongs, etc.
■ (on subsequent recordings) use of **non-western melodic instruments**

Weather Report - Foremost Fusion Band of the 1970's

❑ formed in 1971 by:

■ **Wayne Shorter** (1933 -   ) - tenor sax
■ **Joe Zawinul** (1932-   ) - keyboards/composer

❑ both Shorter and Zawinul were associated with Miles Davis during the 1960's
❑ their new band, **Weather Report,** took off where Davis left off and proceeded to establish the direction that fusion would take during the 1970's
❑ the stylistic characteristics of Weather Report were at first modeled after Miles Davis:

■ modal and/or free jazz improvisations accompanied by electronic textures and rock/funk drumming patterns
■ collective, textural improvisation focus along with featured solos
■ use of amplified and/or distorted keyboard sound textures
■ use of amplified acoustic bass
■ added percussion - Latin-American instruments (congas, cowbells, etc.)

John McLaughlin (1942 -   ) - guitar
and the Mahavishnu Orchestra

- ❏ British rock guitarist who was featured on Miles Davis's landmark *Bitches Brew* album, formed his own fusion band in 1971, The Mahavishnu Orchestra
- ❏ unlike Weather Report which focused on spontaneous, free-form improvisation jams, McLaughlin's band featured tight, high-energy ensemble playing and virtuosic, bebop-based improvisations
- ❏ McLaughlin's guitar had the sound and texture of rock
- ❏ his rapid, bebop lines influenced a new generation of young, rock guitarists and the Mahavishnu Orchestra stepped in to fill the huge void left by the tragic death of Jimi Hendrix in 1971

Herbie Hancock (1940 -   ) - The Synthesizer Revolution in Fusion

- ❏ emerged in the 1970's as a pioneer in new keyboard synthesizer technology.
- ❏ Musically, Hancock was more aligned with the funk movement of the 1970's, a direction that Miles Davis was originally attracted to, but moved away from after the *Bitches Brew* album.
- ❏ drawing on the music of Sly and the Family Stone, George Clinton, The Parliaments, James Brown, Stevie Wonder, etc., Hancock molded a new approach to fusion by:

  - ■ combining funk music and improvisation with
  - ■ high-tech sounds of new keyboard synthesizer technology

A Comparison of Early 1970's Fusion Styles:
Weather Report and Herbie Hancock

	Weather Report	**Herbie Hancock**
improvisations	modal and/or free form; usually textural in nature	modal-based, traditionally constructed melodic lines
use of electronics	distorted electric piano; electronics used as textural sound-effects; distortion of familiar musical sounds explored	synthesizer used to create familiar sound textures; orchestral approach; distortion of traditional musical sounds avoided
arrangements	not emphasized: focus on spontaneous, free-form improvisation - jam session approach	tightly controlled, arranged and polished performance; lack of spontaneous jamming
studio recordings	a snapshot of how the band would sound in live performance	the album itself became the art form; live performance aspects not necessarily considered in making the recording
influences	Miles Davis, John Coltrane, free jazz movement	Miles Davis, Sly & the Family Stone, funk movement
popularity	sold-out concerts and albums consistently selling in the hundreds of thousands	albums consistently sold in the hundreds of thousands; opening act for touring funk bands

Weather Report After 1975 - A New Direction for Fusion

As the turbulent years of the Viet Nam War and civil unrest gave way to the mellow years of the "me generation" of the late 1970's, so did the free jazz/free-form style of fusion give way to a more mellow, traditional-based style. Once again, Weather Report led the way as the sound of fusion changed dramatically after 1975:

A Comparison of Pre-1975 Fusion and Post 1975 Fusion

	Pre-1975	Post 1975
improvisations	modal and/or free-form; usually textural in nature	lyrical improvisations; a return to traditional melodic/bebop lines
use of electronics	distorted electric piano; electronics used as textural sound-effects; distortion of familiar musical sounds explored	synthesizer used to create familiar sound textures; orchestral approach; distortion of traditional musical sounds avoided
compositions	spontaneous improvisations; some pre-planned ideas; mostly sketchy outlines of tunes	carefully-crafted compositions with traditional form & structure
studio recordings	a snapshot of how the band would sound in live performance; artistic considerations were never compromised	deliberate attempts by artists to reach a larger audience; as in the Swing Era, certain artistic compromises were made to ensure commercial success
popularity	sold-out concerts and albums consistently selling in the hundreds of thousands	high record sales, often among the top 100 selling albums; radio airplay; sold-out concerts
important artists	Miles Davis, Weather Report, Mahavishnu Orchestra	Herbie Hancock, Weather Report, Miles Davis, Spyro Gyra, Steps Ahead

❑ in 1975, electric bassist **Jaco Pastorius (1951-1987)** joined Weather Report and was a leading force in the changing sounds of fusion:

- utilized guitar playing techniques on the electric bass
- played ultra-high harmonics on the electric bass (common on the guitar)
- utilized electronic devices, such as a phase shifter and/or chorus effect, to create melodious sounds on the electric bass

❑ the combination of harmonics and electronics enabled Pastorius to

- play lead melodic lines in the same range as a guitar, or saxophone
- provide the band a new lead voice to go along with Wayne Shorter's tenor sax and Joe Zawinul's synthesizers.

❏ at times, Pastorius:

- played ultra-high melodic lines on the electric bass while Zawinul supplied traditional bass lines on the synthesizer.
- played traditional bass lines on his electric bass enabling Zawinul to play lead lines on the synthesizer.

❏ the sound of Weather Report changed considerably after 1975:

- mellower, lighter playing
- avoidance of distorted electronic sounds
- a return to traditional, melodic solo improvisations
- acoustic piano playing by Zawinul - a return to past traditions
- focus on well-produced, commercially accessible recordings; a deliberate attempt to reach a larger audience

Steps Ahead
featuring
Michael Brecker (1949 -   ) - tenor saxophone

Michael Brecker is considered one of the best tenor saxophonists of the fusion era. His improvisatory style was greatly influenced by John Coltrane and he recorded a tribute album to Coltrane in the early 1990's. During the 1980's, Brecker joined forces with a former bebop vibraphonist, **Mike Mainieri (1938 -   )** to form a new fusion band in the early 1980's, **Steps Ahead.** While recording and performing with Steps Ahead, Brecker developed new technological advances in saxophone playing that involved the merging of digital delays, tape loops, and computer-based **MIDI** (**M**usical **I**nstrument **D**igital **I**nterface) technology.

Using these new techniques, Brecker was able to play duets with himself using a MIDI controller wired into his saxophone and mouthpiece, as well as create block-chord harmonies by using immediate digital sample playbacks of his own saxophone - all on an instrument that acoustically produces only one sound at a time.

Miles Davis and Hip Hop Jazz

The last studio recording made by Miles Davis, **DooBop,** featured hip hop rhythms, digital samples and rap vocals by **Easy Mo Bee.**

···
"When young Easy and Miles the Legend got into the studio and started working, the feeling was wonderful. Easy would lay down the tracks; Miles would listen. And when he was happy with what he heard, he'd get out his horn, go to the mike and kick out the melody like he had been practicing those lines for years."
—Gordon Meltzer, liner notes to *DooBop*
···

One more time, Miles showed the way for a new jazz style that continues to emerge during the 1990's - **hip hop jazz.**

(Miles Davis died in the hospital of a stroke on September 28, 1991)

14. Neoclassicism and Post-Modern Bop

By the early 1990's, jazz settled into a "center of gravity" - the bebop/cool jazz period of the 1950's and early 1960's. Led by young musicians such as Wynton Marsalis, Terrence Blanchard, and Joshua Redman, a new era of jazz emerged whereby the music, for the first time in its history, was rooted firmly in a thirty year-old style. Their music was referred to as **post-modern bop,** or **neoclassic bebop.**

During the late 1980's, Miles Davis and Wynton Marsalis widened the gap between the young neoclassics and the fusion/free jazz establishment through several highly-publicized debates in the press. Davis considered anything older than 6 months to be out of fashion, and he criticized Marsalis for playing music that was hopelessly irrelevant. Marsalis counter-charged Davis for selling-out to commercialism and stated that the last time Miles Davis played meaningful jazz was in the early 1960's. After a thirty-year relationship with Columbia Records, Miles Davis left the company in 1987, accusing them of putting more financial support in promoting Marsalis' records (also a Columbia artist) than they were putting into his own - Marsalis was out-selling Miles by the mid-1980's. Davis's last albums were released on the Warner Brothers label.

> "As I see it, the avant-gard has been studiously aligning itself with mainstream jazz for some time. The resurgence of jazz means, in large measure, the resurgence of swing, melody, and beauty, as well as other vintage jazz qualities such as virtuosity, wit, and structure. They are, in effect, going home again."
> —Gary Giddins, jazz critic

> "The basic repertoire of today's jazz .... Looks back more than ahead."
> —Donald Megill, jazz author

Wynton Marsalis (1961 -   ) - trumpet

- Wynton Marsalis was the primary leader in the rise of the post-modern bebop style, or neoclassicism in jazz
- attended Julliard School of Music in 1979 (as did Miles Davis 35 years earlier); became a virtuoso classical trumpet player to go along with his first-rate jazz improvisation abilities
- first recorded with Art Blakey and the Jazz Messengers in 1981, followed by tours with Herbie Hancock and his own band in 1982
- Marsalis is outspoken about the legacy of past jazz styles and his early performances with Blakey and Hancock reflect the straight-ahead bebop/cool period of the 1950's and early 1960's
- his speaking out for the acceptance of jazz as America's classical music created

67

much controversy among those who were looking ahead for new directions in jazz, not to the past

•••

"In his quest to legitimize jazz, he blasted other jazz styles that did not fit his mainstream definition."

—Paul Tanner, jazz author

•••

Joshua Redman (1969 -   ) - tenor sax

Son of avant-gard saxophonist, Dewey Redman, Joshua's career as a jazz artist almost didn't happen; his 4.0 high school grade point average landed him at Harvard University in the pre-med program in 1987. However, his musical training and ties to the jazz tradition through his father, led him to various playing opportunities in Boston during summer breaks.

After graduating from Harvard in 1991, Summa Cum Laude and Phi Beta Kappa, Joshua entered the Thelonius Monk International Jazz Saxophone Competition and won the event which led to his first recording contract and a thriving career as a jazz artist.

His playing style is centered in post modern bop/neoclassical jazz; strong elements of Sonny Rollins and Cannonball Adderley can be heard in his playing - he seems less influenced by John Coltrane than other contemporary saxophonists.

II. Listening
Examples

1. Introduction

(No Examples)

2. Roots of Jazz

| Example 1 |

HENRY RATCLIFF

Louisiana (196?, Parchman Penitentiary, Mississippi)

BAKARI-BADJI

Field Song from Senegal- (196?, Senegal)
from the New World Recordings album, *Roots Of The Blues*

Recording Notes

❑ Smithsonian Institute field recordings by Alan Lomax and David Sapir

    1. Mississippi prisoner picking cotton; song of freedom
    2. peanut farmer in Senegal (West Africa)

❑ similar characteristics between the two recordings include:

- free rhythmic feel (lack of a steady tempo); syncopated vocal lines
- generally, descending melodic lines (with peaks and valleys in between)
- sliding, "liquid" vocal style (the opposite of the trained operatic voice)
- rough, nasal vocal sound
- spontaneous "feel" to the music

Example 2

TANGLE EYE AND PRISONERS

No More, My Lord (unknown date, Parchman Penitentiary, Mississippi)
from the New World Recordings album, *Roots Of The Blues*

Recording Notes

❏ Smithsonian field recording - **WORK SONG** example
❏ Tangle Eye (nickname of the "lead" singer) and a group of Mississippi chain gang workers singing while chopping wood
❏ musical characteristics include:

- lead vocalist with everyone else following Tangle Eye's lead vocal
- generally, descending melodic lines
- use of simple vocal harmony
- sliding, or "liquid" vocal quality
- nasal vocal sound
- axes fall on weak beats - very slow tempo (difficult labor)
- intense, passionate performance; spontaneous in nature

Example 3

REVEREND CRENSHAW
AND THE CONGREGATION OF NEW BROWN'S CHAPEL

Lining Hymn and Prayer (196?, Memphis, Tennessee)
from the New World Recordings album, _Roots Of The Blues_

Recording Notes

❏ Smithsonian field recording: Lining Hymn & Prayer, religious service
❏ musical characteristics include:

- each word of the hymn is elongated, stretched-out, and changed from the original European source
- call & response between the minister and congregation (the origins of doo-wop)
- use of short, repeated melodic lines - Riffs
- sliding, "liquid" vocal style
- nasal vocal quality
- intensive use of vocal effects by the minister to get his point across (you will immediately hear where James Brown developed his style)

Example 4

ROBERT JOHNSON

Hellhound On My Trail - (1937, Dallas)
from the Columbia album, *Robert Johnson: The Complete Recordings*

Recording Notes

- ❏ superb example of country or rural blues
- ❏ A - A - B blues lyric and musical form
- ❏ each phrase has a different length due to the variations in the lyrics
- ❏ sliding, "liquid" vocal style; use of scoops, smears, and bent notes, or blues notes
- ❏ nasal vocal quality
- ❏ voice & guitar call & response: Johnson uses the guitar in two ways:

    1. solid rhythmical accompaniment - strong 4-beat strumming
    2. at the end of his vocal phrases, he stops strumming and plays a melodic figure as if to extend the melody with the guitar

- ❏ local, folk lyrics: use of Southern slang

Example 5

BESSIE SMITH

Cold In Hand Blues - (1925, New York)
from the Time-Life recording, *Louis Armstrong*

featured musicians:
Bessie Smith - vocalist
Louis Armstrong - cornet
Fred Longshaw - piano

Recording Notes

- ❏ classic example of urban or city blues
- ❏ begins with a non-blues verse (common for most vaudeville popular songs)
- ❏ *12-bar A - A - B blues form* begins after the opening verse
- ❏ powerful vocal style; Bessie Smith was a nationally-known vaudeville star who toured the country performing the blues in large theaters without amplification
- ❏ use of vibrato clear enunciation of words; full vocal tone (nearly the opposite Robert Johnson)
- ❏ blues notes are evident throughout, although they are sung without the sliding, or "liquid" sound of country blues
- ❏ cornetist Louis Armstrong answers her vocal lines with his own improvisations

Example 6

SCOTT JOPLIN (PIANO ROLL)

Maple Leaf Rag - (recorded in 1974 on a 1910 Steinway player piano) from the album boxed-set, *The Smithsonian Collection of Classic Jazz*

Recording Notes

- ❑ *Maple Leaf Rag* was composed in 1899
- ❑ *Maple Leaf Rag* form: **A-A - B-B - A - C-C - D-D** (four primary themes) (each letter represents a different 16-bar melody)
- ❑ typical right hand 3-note melodic patterns
- ❑ typical left hand 2-beat march-like rhythms
- ❑ thoroughly composed - no improvisation
- ❑ use of multiple melodies played simultaneously, or **Counterpoint**
- ❑ complex musical form (see above)

Example 7

ERNEST "PUNCH" MILLER BAND

Tiger Rag - (1962, New Orleans)
from the Atlantic Album, *New Orleans*

featured musicians:
Ernest "Punch" Miller - trumpet
George Lewis - cornet
Fred Longshaw - piano
Louis Nelson - trombone
Emanuel Sayles - banjo
Papa John Joseph - bass
Abbey Foster - drums

Recording Notes

❑ re-creation of a New Orleans funeral parade band (on the way back from the funeral site)

❑ several of the musicians on this recording played in Storyville including Papa John Joseph and Abbey Foster

❑ use of **counterpoint** (multiple) melodies played simultaneously:

■ trumpet plays the primary melody, or tune
■ trombone improvises a low melody
■ clarinet improvises an upper melody

❑ drummer Abbey Foster plays a swinging, syncopated *march beat*

❑ use of the banjo for harmonic support (pianos are not used in marching bands!)

Example 8

TURK MURPHY BAND

Maple Leaf Rag - (1971, San Francisco)
from the Atlantic Album, *New Orleans*

featured musicians:
Turk Murphy - trombone
Leon Oakley - cornet
Phil Howe - clarinet
Pete Clute - piano
Carl Lunsford - banjo
Jim Maihack - tuba
Thad Vanden - drums

Recording Notes

❑ re-creation of a New Orleans/Storyville "brothel band" (actually, few Storyville brothels hired bands; most jazz was played in bars and nightclubs)
❑ piano adds harmonic support for improvisation making the banjo's role more rhythmic than harmonic
❑ original melody of Maple Leaf Rag is paraphrased (altered but not beyond recognition)
❑ three-part counterpoint (multiple melodies):

■ trumpet - primary melody (tune)
■ trombone - improvised lower melody
■ clarinet - improvised upper melody

❑ drummer Thad Vanden plays syncopated, swinging marching patterns
❑ the rhythmic flow of this version of Maple Leaf Rag is less "ragged" than Joplin's original

3. Early Jazz - New Orleans Style

> **Example 9**
>
>
>
> # THE ORIGINAL DIXIELAND JASS BAND
>
> ***Dixie Jazz Band One-Step*** - (1917, New York)
> from the RCA Victor album, *The Original Dixieland Jass Band*
>
> **featured musicians:**
> **Nick LaRocca** - cornet
> **Larry Shields** - clarinet
> **Eddie Edwards** - trombone
> **Henry Ragas** - piano
> **Tony Spargo** - drums

Recording Notes

❏ this was the *first instrumental jazz recording; Dixie Jazz Band One-Step* introduced jazz to millions of people who had never heard this kind of music

❏ the musicians perform this music as a novelty, mocking New Orleans jazz, rather than treating it with respect

❏ clarinet shrieks, comical trombone swoops, trumpet "horse whinnies," and other "barnyard" effects are obvious

❏ the music sounds pre-planned and well-rehearsed with **very little spontaneity or improvisation;** Victor was selling records to a "sophisticated" audience who expected "first-rate" performances

❏ this music resembles ragtime more than jazz (ragtime was the point of reference for the musicians' interpretation of *Dixie Jazz Band One-Step*)

JOE "KING" OLIVER AND THE CREOLE JAZZ BAND

Dippermouth Blues - (1923 Chicago)
from the Time-Life recording, *Louis Armstrong*

featured musicians:
Joe Oliver - cornet (soloist)
Louis Armstrong - 2nd cornet
Johnny Dodds - clarinet
Kid Ory - trombone
Lil Hardin - piano
Warren "Baby" Dodds - drums

Recording Notes

❑ composed by Oliver for Louis Armstrong who was affectionately called "Dippermouth" by his friends because of his large, infectious smile
❑ this music contains the vitality and passion missing in the previous Original Dixieland Jass Band recording
❑ 4-part **collective improvisation**

- Oliver: primary melody
- Armstrong: secondary melody (improvised)
- Dodds: high melody (improvised)
- Ory: low melody (improvised)

❑ short solo space for Oliver; the focus of New Orleans jazz had been **collective improvisation** (unlike contemporary jazz which focuses on solo improvisation)
❑ strong, 4-beat rhythmic feel derived from the blues tradition
❑ swinging style is different from the "ragged" feeling of ragtime (e.g. Original Dixieland Jass Band)

Example 11

LOUIS ARMSTRONG HOT FIVE

Gut Bucket Blues - (1925, Chicago)
from the Columbia album, *The Hot Fives, Vol. 1*

featured musicians:
Louis Armstrong - cornet/vocal introductions
Johnny Dodds - clarinet
Kid Ory - trombone
Lil (Hardin) Armstrong - piano
Johnny St. Cyr - banjo

Recording Notes

❏ first commercial recording of the Hot Five
❏ 12-bar blues tune (A - A - B form)
❏ new performance element: each player has a featured solo
❏ each soloist is introduced by Armstrong (Armstrong's solo is introduced by Kid Ory)
❏ the focus moves away from collective improvisation to solo improvisation
❏ Armstrong's solo flows along without dependence on ragtime phrasing; he is defining the swing feel in jazz

Example 12

LOUIS ARMSTRONG HOT FIVE

Heebie Jeebies (1926, Chicago)
from the Columbia Album, *The Hot Fives, Vol. 1*

featured musicians:
Louis Armstrong - cornet/vocalist
Johnny Dodds - clarinet
Kid Ory - trombone
Lil (Hardin) Armstrong - piano
Johnny St. Cyr - banjo

Recording Notes

❏ noted for Armstrong's **"scat"** vocal solo; first time scat singing was heard on a commercial recording

- scat singing: jazz vocal improvisation using nonsense syllables instead of words
- scat singing has been used throughout the years after this recording by both popular and jazz vocalists (Ella Fitzgerald, Bing Crosby, Frank Sinatra, etc.)

❏ Armstrong had developed his scat singing technique as a youngster in New Orleans, singing on street corners trying to imitate the instruments of the brass bands

Example 13

LOUIS ARMSTRONG HOT FIVE

Cornet Chop Suey (1926, Chicago)
from the Columbia album, *The Hot Fives, Vol. 1*

featured musicians:
Louis Armstrong - cornet
Johnny Dodds - clarinet
Kid Ory - trombone
Lil (Hardin) Armstrong - piano
Johnny St. Cyr - banjo

Recording Notes

❏ radical departure from the collective improvisation-based New Orleans jazz style

❏ except for a short piano solo by Lil Armstrong, Louis is featured throughout the piece as a soloist; the band is heard sparingly

❏ virtuosity is set to a high level by Armstrong; he handles a difficult composition (his own) with a command of the cornet unsurpassed by previous jazz performers

❏ this recording marked the beginning of solo improvisation as the primary focus in jazz - a move away from collective improvisation

❏ this was the first recording of an extended jazz solo improvisation

Example 14

LOUIS ARMSTRONG AND HIS HOT FIVE

West End Blues (1928, Chicago)
from the Columbia album, *Louis Armstrong Story, Vol. 1*

featured musicians:
Louis Armstrong - cornet/scat vocal
Earl "Fatha" Hines - piano
Jimmy Strong - clarinet
Fred Robinson - trombone
Mancy Cara - banjo
Zutty Singleton - drums

Recording Notes

"A great moment in 20th century music."
—John Chilton, jazz historian

"...summarized the past and predicted the future."
—Gunther Schuller, musician, conductor, author

"We cannot date the birth of jazz as an art music after these heroic notes."
—J.R. Taylor, jazz critic, author

❏ long considered Armstrong's masterpiece; a milestone in the development of jazz that gave the music its definitive character
❏ brilliant opening **cadenza** - solo; forecasts the modern age of jazz and bebop
❏ 12-bar blues form
❏ subtle scat duet with clarinetist Jimmy Strong
❏ creative piano solo by Earl "Fatha" Hines makes the final break away from the "bonds of ragtime"
❏ Hines' solo features horn-like lines in the right hand, with a relaxed non-ragtime (stride) left hand accompaniment
❏ last chorus is a classic with Armstrong's "bravura" trumpet playing and syncopated improvisation over the top of the band

Example 15

SIDNEY BECHET

Blue Horizon - (New York, 1940)
from the album boxed-set, *The Smithsonian Collection of Classic Jazz*

featured musicians:
Sidney Bechet - clarinet
Sidney de Paris - trumpet
Manzie Johnson - drums

Recording Notes

❑ Bechet, playing the clarinet in the same manner as he did in New Orleans 25 years earlier, was a master of constructing solos

❑ blues-drenched performance; Bechet was "singing" the blues through his clarinet

❑ each chorus of **12-bar blues** builds in intensity; just as he seems to have reached a peak, along comes another, more intense chorus

❑ extensive use of **vocalistic effects** on the clarinet

■ scoops
■ soaring notes
■ wailing high notes
■ intense bent notes, or blues notes
■ wide vibrato - very emotional

❑ notice the drummer, Manzie Johnson, playing military press rolls instead of traditional jazz patterns; a throwback to the brass band tradition of Storyville

4. Chicago Jazz

| Example 16 |

FRANKIE TRUMBAUER ORCHESTRA

Singin' The Blues (1927, Chicago)
from the Time-Life album, *Bix Beiderbecke*

featured musicians:
Frankie Trumbauer - C-melody sax
Bix Beiderbecke - cornet
Jimmy Dorsey - clarinet

Recording Notes

❏ both Trumbauer and Beiderbecke exhibit a subtle, cool approach in their music; this is reflective in nature, not outgoing like the New Orleans/Louis Armstrong approach

❏ Trumbauer utilizes unusual intervals (wider skips in between notes) in his solo

❏ Beiderbecke incorporates several **"tri-tone"** intervals in his solo - an advanced harmonic concept commonly found in the **Impressionistic** music of **Ravel** and **Debussy**

❏ Beiderbecke's invention, **"the rip,"** an aggressive technique that he effectively used in contrast with his usual subtle approach, is a highlight of his solo

❏ Beiderbecke's solo was later transcribed by bandleader **Fletcher Henderson** who had his entire trumpet section play it note for note in his arrangement of *Singin' The Blues*

BIX BEIDERBECKE AND HIS GANG

Jazz Me Blues (1927, Chicago)
from the Time-Life album, *Bix Beiderbecke*

featured musicians:
Bix Beiderbecke - cornet
Don Murray - clarinet
Adrian Rollini- bass saxophone

Recording Notes

❑ despite its title, *Jazz Me Blues* is not a blues song and does not follow the A-A-B blues form
❑ Beiderbecke's 8-note break in the middle of his solo became one of the most imitated licks in jazz
❑ as Fletcher Henderson had done with *Singin' The Blues*, bandleader **Bob Crosby** transcribed Beiderbecke's solo on *Jazz Me Blues* and had his trumpet section play it note for note in his arrangement
❑ collective improvisation on last chorus acknowledges the New Orleans tradition

BIX BEIDERBECKE

In A Mist - (1927, New York)
from the Time-Life album, *Bix Beiderbecke*

featured musician:
Bix Beiderbecke - solo piano

Recording Notes

❑ the only known recording of Beiderbecke's piano playing
❑ an important example demonstrating the idea of merging elements of classical and jazz music together in creating a new approach (now referred to as **Third Stream Jazz**)
❑ **George Gershwin** brought jazz elements and the blues into his classical compositions such as *Rhapsody In Blue* and *Piano Concerto in F*
❑ Beiderbecke brings classical music elements into jazz with similar, unique results
❑ the melodic lines contain such Impressionistic elements as **whole tone** and **octatonic** (diminished) scales - ideas left unexplored by jazz musicians until the 1950's
❑ harmonically, *In A Mist* is full of chromatic shifts and tri-tone chord substitutions - at least 15 years before pianists used these devices on a regular basis in jazz
❑ obviously, this recording created a sensation among jazz musicians who marveled at the harmonic complexity and skillful construction of the composition

5. Stride Piano

Example 19

JELLY ROLL MORTON

Maple Leaf Rag (Washington, D.C., 1938)
from the album boxed-set, *The Smithsonian Collection of Classic Jazz*

Recording Notes

- ❑ Morton jazzes-up the original melody without losing sight of it entirely (also called **melodic paraphrasing)**
- ❑ Jelly Roll changes the left hand accompaniment to fit the rhythmic syncopation of the melody in the right hand
- ❑ instead of sounding "ragged," Jelly Roll makes his version of *Maple Leaf Rag* swing
- ❑ notice the "walking," or striding, left-hand bass lines; they flow naturally with the right-hand melodies
- ❑ this later recording represents classic **New Orleans stride** piano style - performed by its inventor

Example 20

JAMES P. JOHNSON

You've Got To Be Modernistic (1930, New York)
from the Affinity album, *Piano Portraits, Vol. 1*

Recording Notes

- ❑ this recording shows the virtuosity of Johnson with his hard-driving left hand patterns supporting his rapid right hand improvisations
- ❑ notice the striding (walking) left-hand bass patterns
- ❑ his solo contains complex harmonies with tri-tone and chromatic chord substitutions - a forerunner to bebop
- ❑ use of **syncopated riffs** to build musical intensity
- ❑ judging by this performance, it is not difficult to imagine Johnson as the winner of nearly every cutting contest he entered

Example 21

EARL "FATHA" HINES

Memories of You (1974, live - Hot Club d'Orange: Orange, France)
from the Black & Blue album, *Live in Orange*

Recording Notes

- ❑ recorded later in his career (he was 70 at the time), Hines creates a mini-piano sonata out of this old popular song (composed by stride pianist Eubie Blake)
- ❑ after stating the melody out of tempo, Hines paraphrases the tune in a slow, soulful **New Orleans stride** style before launching into his improvisations
- ❑ by the fourth chorus, he switches gears, picks up the temp, and launches into a virtuosic, complex **Harlem stride**-influenced improvisation
- ❑ after reaching an obvious climactic point, he returns to the original melody and New Orleans soulful style before ending the tune with a full-blown classical **coda** (ending)
- ❑ the last chord is a blues chord
- ❑ you can hear Hines humming throughout the piece as if he were trying to get the piano to bend, scoop, slide and smear notes (the piano is literally an extension of his voice)

Example 22

FATS WALLER

I Ain't Got Nobody - (1937, New York)
from the album boxed-set, *The Smithsonian Collection of Classic Jazz*

Recording Notes

- ❑ although Waller did not compose this song, he made it his own composition through his soulful interpretation
- ❑ Waller was an important transition figure between stride and modern piano styles
- ❑ although this is a slow song, the intensity of the stride style slowly builds with each chorus
- ❑ while the left-hand walking stride lines are present, they are much less intrusive with his bluesy right-hand melodic lines
- ❑ his left-hand activity is not as complex as other stride pianists (especially his teacher, James P. Johnson)
- ❑ listen to the **"funky"** style that emerges half-way into the song; this forecasts the rolling piano style of rock and roll music by almost 20 years

Example 23

MEADE "LUX" LEWIS

Honky Tonk Train - (New York, 1937)
from the album boxed-set, *The Smithsonian Collection of Classic Jazz*

Recording Notes

- ❑ as with most boogie woogie tunes, this is a **12-bar blues**
- ❑ notice the **left-hand driving, walking bass riffs**
- ❑ the **bluesy right-hand melodic riffs** are quite syncopated and build in intensity with each chorus
- ❑ this tune was re-worked in 1956 by **Bill Doggett** into an early rock and roll instrumental hit, *Honky Tonk*

Example 24

ART TATUM

I Know That You Know (1949, live - Shrine Auditorium, Los Angeles)
from the Columbia album, *Piano Starts Here*

Recording Notes

- ❑ live concert performance; one of the few formal concerts performed by the legendary Art Tatum (his career was largely spent in small piano bars and jazz clubs)
- ❑ tempo of *I Know That You Know* is clocked at 450 beats per minute:

  - ■ 1,000 notes per minute
  - ■ 17 notes per second

- ❑ notice the virtuosity of the left hand: plays the walking bass patterns of stride as well as the chord above the bass notes; all with just the left hand!
- ❑ the right hand jets around the keys with amazing ease; it never sounds as if he's "on the edge"
- ❑ despite the rapid tempo, his melodic lines gracefully flow along, creating music that rises above the virtuosic technique
- ❑ part-way into the performance, he slows down and plays as funky as Fats Waller before "tearing up" the ending

91

6. The Swing Era or Big Band Era

JELLY ROLL MORTON AND HIS RED HOT PEPPERS

Black Bottom Stomp - (1926, New York)
from the album boxed-set, *The Smithsonian Collection of Classic Jazz*

featured musicians:
Jelly Roll Morton - piano / composer / arranger
George Mitchell - trumpet
Omer Simeon - clarinet
Kid Ory - trombone
Johnny St. Cyr - banjo
Andrew Hilaire - drums

Recording Notes

❑ this composition is in 2 parts:

    A. focuses on a conversation between written and improvised parts (a call & response idea)
    B. focuses on solo improvisation with various combinations of accompanying instruments playing written parts

❑ the two parts are bridged by a short **interlude**
❑ the whole composition features built-in solo breaks, stop-time rhythmic cues, and frequent use of rhythmic tension (extensively syncopated lines)
❑ the 2nd section is repeated seven times with six different instrument combinations

Black Bottom Stomp Schematic

INTRO......... full ensemble (collective improvisation)
A1 .... full ensemble (written)
A2 .... trumpet / ensemble call & response (improvised / written)
A3 .... clarinet and banjo
                 ** INTERLUDE - modulation **
B1 .... full ensemble / trumpet & trombone / full ensemble
B2 .... clarinet solo /full ensemble (call and response)
B3 .... piano solo / full ensemble (call and response)
B4 .... trumpet solo with stop-time rhythmic accompaniment
B5 .... banjo solo with 4-beat walking string bass line
B6 .... full ensemble / drum solo /full ensemble
B7 .... shout chorus: full ensemble with tom tom drum beat; also includes a brief .... trombone solo break
CODA (end) collective improvisation (short - 2 measures)

Example 26

FLETCHER HENDERSON ORCHESTRA

The Stampede (1926, New York)
from the album boxed-set, *The Smithsonian Collection of Classic Jazz*

featured musicians:
Coleman Hawkins - tenor sax
Rex Stewart - trumpet
Fletcher Henderson - piano

Recording Notes

❑ this recording displays many of the innovative techniques in big band writing that were introduced by Fletcher Henderson
❑ you can hear many examples of the **saxes pitted against the brass,** tossing melodic riffs back and forth
❑ brilliant improvised solos by Hawkins and Stewart, often backed with written horn parts
❑ a short **saxophone soli** occurs between the tenor sax solo and the trumpet solo
❑ the **shout chorus** occurs near the end of the piece

Example 27

BENNY GOODMAN ORCHESTRA

Don't Be That Way - (1938, live - Carnegie Hall, New York)
from the Columbia album, *Greatest Hits*

featured musicians:
Benny Goodman - clarinet
Harry James - trumpet
Babe Russin - tenor sax
Vernon Brown - trombone
Gene Krupa - drums

Recording Notes

❏ judging by the reaction of the audience, some of whom paid top dollar to sit behind the band on stage, Goodman had not lost any of his popularity in the 2.5 years since the famed Los Angeles Palomar Theater performance that launched his career in 1935

❏ this band was loud; the solos were hot;

❏ notice the twist on the shout chorus as it gets softer and softer instead of louder and more intense

❏ Gene Krupa was a maniac drummer - his hair flew in all directions and he had a "greasy," rebellious look - the forerunner to teenage rebellion in the 1950s

❏ features excellent improvisations by Goodman, James, Russin, and Brown

Example 28

BENNY GOODMAN SEXTET

Seven Come Eleven - (1939, New York)
from the Charlie Christian Columbia album, *Solo Flight*

featured musicians:
Benny Goodman - clarinet
Charlie Christian - electric guitar
Lionel Hampton - vibraphone
Fletcher Henderson - piano
Artie Bernstein - bass
Nick Fatool - drums

Recording Notes

❏ riff tune composed by Charlie Christian
❏ precise, tight-sounding ensemble - **chamber jazz**
❏ focus on brilliant solos by Christian, Hampton and Goodman
❏ use of riffs to accompany soloists

- vibraphone riff is played behind Christian's guitar
- clarinet and guitar riff played behind Hampton's vibraphone solo

....

"We just faked it. I started out. Artie Bernstein came in on bass. Hampton and Charlie Christian came in with a riff - Charlie was a real young kid then, but he was great - and Benny came in. And that's how it happened!"
> —Nick Fatool, drummer (from *The Guitarists* liner notes
> by Marty Grosz and Lawrence Cohn)

....

Example 29

Duke Ellington and His Cotton Club Orchestra

The Mooche - (1928, New York)
from the Time-Life album, *Duke Ellington*

featured musicians:
Duke Ellington - piano
Barney Bigard - clarinet
Bubber Miley - muted trumpet
Johnny Hodges - alto sax

Recording Notes

- ❏ originally a dance number for the Cotton Club show
- ❏ Ellington honed his composition and arranging skills in making the music fit the Cotton Club's jungle theme with dense textures of instruments and melancholy melodic lines
- ❏ early examples of Ellington's **cross-section voicing techniques** (e.g. scoring a chord between the saxes and the trombones instead of just the saxes or just the trombones)
- ❏ *The Mooche* is *not* in the form of the blues *except* where improvisations occur; each soloist plays over the 12-bar A-A-B minor blues form
- ❏ Ellington took advantage of Bubber Miley's **muting** techniques on the trumpet in creating a **"growling style"**
- ❏ Ellington was a master of portraying the black culture through his music, always bringing out specific feelings and responses from his listeners:

"I feel in this piece a conflict of two elemental forces: (1) the violence of nature, which is an eternal struggle with the other (2) the force of man, a more melancholy, restrained, and mental force."

—Dutch critic review; from the *Duke Ellington* album liner notes by Dan Morgenstern

Example 30

DUKE ELLINGTON ORCHESTRA

It Don't Mean A Thing If It Ain't Got That Swing - (1932, New York)
from the Time-Life album, *Duke Ellington*

featured musicians:
Duke Ellington - piano / composer / arranger
Ivey Anderson - vocalist
Joe "Tricky Sam" Nanton - growl trombone
Johnny Hodges - alto sax
Cootie Williams - muted trumpet

Recording Notes

❏ every swing-era big band featured a vocalist - including Duke Ellington
❏ Ellington utilized Ivey Anderson beyond her normal role of singing popular songs with the band:

- Anderson's voice is further utilized as another musical instrument in the band
- her scat singing was pre-planned by Ellington and scored in his arrangement of *It Don't Mean A Thing...*

❏ Ellington was fascinated with **mutes** - devices placed in the bell of a brass instrument (trumpet or trombone) to alter its tone:
❏ Cootie Williams and Joe Nanton achieve human voice-like sounds by using plunger and wah-wah mutes

Example 31

DUKE ELLINGTON ORCHESTRA

Concerto For Cootie - (1940, New York)
from the Time-Life album, *Duke Ellington*

featured musicians:
Cootie Williams - trumpet soloist
Duke Ellington - piano / composer / arrangement

Recording Notes

❑ Ellington composed this piece as a "showcase" for Cootie Williams (later on, lyrics were added by Bob Russell and the name of the composition became *Do Nothin' Till You Hear From Me*)

❑ extensive use of **mutes** called for in the piece

  ■ plunger mute over a straight mute
  ■ plunger mute over an open bell
  ■ normal tone: un-muted

❑ the **classical concerto form** remains intact as Ellington condensed the piece into a three-minute performance

Concerto for Cootie Schematic

INTRODUCTION
A1: 10-bar theme (muted trumpet)
A2: repeat of A theme with melodic variation
B: 2nd theme is 8-bars long (change in mute)
A3: 1st theme repeated with further melodic variation
MODULATION to new key
C: new theme with different feeling / un-muted trumpet
MODULATION to original key
A4: partial statement of 1st theme (6-bars)
CODA - ending consisting of new material

| Example 32 |

DUKE ELLINGTON ORCHESTRA

Harlem Air Shaft - (1940, New York)
from the Time-Life album, *Duke Ellington*

featured musicians:
Cootie Williams - trumpet
Barney Bigard - clarinet

Recording Notes

❏ *Harlem Air Shaft* is loosely based on the 12-bar blues form
❏ this represents one of Ellington's most effective **tone poems**
❏ the shifting moods in the piece tell the story of life in a Harlem apartment building
❏ Ellington's arrangement contains many standard big band scoring techniques including **saxophone soli, call and response** between the saxes and brass, and a driving **shout chorus**
❏ Ellington's use of **cross-section voicings** can be heard extensively throughout the piece
❏ Ellington also uses musical sound effects such as the choked cymbal representing someone banging on the steam pipes for more heat
❏ Ellington offered the following program notes on the sheet music of *Harlem Air Shaft*:

....

"So much goes on in a Harlem air shaft. You get the full essence of Harlem in an air shaft. You hear fights, you smell dinner, you hear people making love. You hear intimate gossip floating down. You hear the radio. An air shaft is one great big loudspeaker. You hear the janitor's dogs. The man upstairs' aerial falls down and breaks your window. You smell coffee. A wonderful thing is that smell. An air shaft has got every contrast. One guy is cooking dried fish and rice and another guy's got a great big turkey. Guy-with-fish's wife is a terrific cooker, but the guy's wife with the turkey is doing a sad job. You hear people praying, fighting, snoring. Jitterbugs are jumping up and down, always over you, never below you. That's a funny thing about jitterbugs. They're always above you. I've tried to put all that in Harlem Air Shaft."

–Duke Ellington, 1940; from the liner notes of the Time-Life album, *Duke Ellington*
....

Example 33

COUNT BASIE ORCHESTRA

One O'Clock Jump - (1937, New York)
from the Time-Life album, *Count Basie*

featured musicians:
Herschel Evans - tenor sax
George Hunt - trombone
Buck Clayton - trumpet
Lester Young - tenor sax
All American-Rhythm Section:
Count Basie - piano
Freddie Green - guitar
Walter Page - bass
Jo Jones - drums

Recording Notes

❏ one of Basie's most popular recordings
❏ this recording reveals the essence of Kansas City swing:

- 12-bar blues form
- riff tune (melody based upon a repeated riff)
- head arrangements (notes stored in the musicians' heads, instead of music paper)
- primary focus on improvisation
- driving rhythm section - very danceable beat

❏ although not clearly heard on the early recordings of the Basie band, the All-American Rhythm Section drives the ensemble with power and energy behind Green's rhythmic guitar strumming, Page's solid walking bass lines, and Jones' explosive drumming
❏ Basie's blues-laced piano provides harmonic support

Example 34

COUNT BASIE ORCHESTRA

Jumpin' At The Woodside - (1938, New York)
from the Time-Life album, *Count Basie*

featured musicians:
Count Basie - piano
Buck Clayton - trumpet
Lester Young - tenor sax
Herschel Evans - clarinet
All American-Rhythm Section

Recording Notes

- ❑ another hit riff tune
- ❑ features Basie's *economical piano style*
- ❑ hard driving beat supplied by The All-American Rhythm Section (especially Jones and Green)
- ❑ terrific solos; Kansas City jazz focused primarily on the improvisation tradition of jazz

---

Example 35

COLEMAN HAWKINS ORCHESTRA

Body And Soul - (1939, New York)
from the album boxed-set, *The Smithsonian Collection of Classic Jazz*

Recording Notes

- ❑ *Body And Soul* was Hawkins' most successful recording, artistically and commercially
- ❑ except for the opening partial statement of the melody, Coleman's performance is entirely improvised with very little interaction with his band
- ❑ sensitive, but outgoing improvisatory character
- ❑ rich, deep, full-bodied, yet sensuous tone quality
- ❑ medium to rapid **vibrato**
- ❑ angular, non-lyrical (non-singable) lines that outline the harmony (harmonic-based improvisation)
- ❑ rhythmically intense playing; Hawkins tends to push the tempo and play on-top-of the beat

Example 36

Count Basie Kansas City Seven

Lester Leaps In (1939, New York)
from the album boxed-set, *The Smithsonian Collection of Classic Jazz*

featured musicians:
Lester Young - tenor sax
Count Basie - piano
All-American Rhythm Section

Recording Notes

❑ an early **rhythm & blues** tune, *Lester Leaps In* is based upon the harmonic structure of George Gershwin's *I Got Rhythm*

❑ Young's sound is quite a bit lighter and more buoyant than Coleman Hawkins

❑ while outgoing in nature, Young allows more space in his solo and the feeling is more relaxed and laid-back

❑ Young's improvised lines tend to follow scale patterns (consecutive notes), rather than outline harmonies; not as angular as Hawkins

❑ very little use of the **vibrato**

❑ classic, dual interplay between Basie and Young near the end of the tune

❑ notice Basie's **economical** piano style; very few notes, but each one swings hard

Example 37

BILLIE HOLIDAY

All Of Me (1941, New York)
from the album boxed-set, *The Smithsonian Collection of Classic Jazz*

featured musicians:
Billie Holiday - vocalist
Lester Young - tenor sax

Recording Notes

❑ *All Of Me* is a representative example of Holiday's vocal style:

■ **melodic paraphrasing**

• changes the melody without losing the original intent

■ **blues note substitutions (bent notes)**

• by lowering, or bending certain notes, the melody takes on a bluesy quality

■ **melismatic phrasing techniques**

• the technique of holding one note longer than usual and then "catching-up" by singing succeeding notes shorter than usual
• this technique was used to perfection by many vocalists such as Frank Sinatra who once stated that he learned everything about vocal phrasing by listening to Billie Holiday

❑ while *All Of Me* is not a blues song, Holiday makes it sound bluesy by using the above vocal techniques
❑ her interpretation of this "upbeat" song takes on a more ominous spin in this recording
❑ notice how Lester Young matches her vocal style and sound through his tenor sax during his short solo

Example 38

ELLA FITZGERALD

You'd Be So Nice To Come Home To (1964, Paris, France)
from the album boxed-set, *The Smithsonian Collection of Classic Jazz*

featured musicians:
Ella Fitzgerald - vocals
Roy Eldridge - trumpet

Recording Notes

- ❑ many examples of **melismatic phrasing** techniques
- ❑ short **scat duet** with Roy Eldridge
- ❑ unlike Louis Armstrong who used nonsense syllables while "scatting," Ella uses the song's regular lyrics in her scat duet
- ❑ **scat** vocal improvisation using the lyrics of the song
- ❑ more than Billie Holiday, Ella improvised new melodies over the harmony much like a jazz horn player
- ❑ this recording also reveals her extraordinary vocal range and accuracy of pitch

7. Modern Jazz - Bebop

> **Example 39**
>
> ## LIONEL HAMPTON ORCHESTRA
>
> ***Hey Ba Ba Re Bop*** - (1946, New York)
> from the Time-Life album, *Your Hit Parade: The Late '40's*
>
> **featured musicians:**
> **Lionel Hampton** - vocals
> **Cat Anderson** - trumpet
> **Herbie Fields** - clarinet
>
>

Recording Notes

- ❏ ten-piece band (smaller version of the swing band) - also known as a **jump band**
- ❏ derived from the swing band tradition
- ❏ 12-bar A-A-B blues form
- ❏ riff-based tune (Kansas City jazz tradition)
- ❏ vocal call & response between Hampton and his band members
- ❏ use of scat lyrics
- ❏ high, screeching, outgoing solos, especially by Cat Anderson
- ❏ hard-driving drumming patterns, excellent for dancing (the model for early rock & roll drumming)
- ❏ *Hey Ba Ba Re Bop* is considered a forerunner of early rock and roll

Example 40

DIZZY GILLESPIE ALL-STAR QUINTET

Shaw 'Nuff - (1945, New York)
from the album boxed-set, *The Smithsonian Collection of Classic Jazz*

featured musicians:
Dizzie Gillespie - trumpet
Charlie Parker - alto sax
Al Haig - piano
Curly Russell - bass
Big Sid Catlett - drums

Recording Notes

❏ this studio recording lacks the spontaneous jam-session approach of live performances

❏ the polished arrangement of *Shaw 'Nuff* suggests a certain amount of rehearsal, rather than a typical bebop jam session

❏ *Shaw 'Nuff* is a new melody line composed by Dizzy Gillespie over the form and structure of the popular George Gershwin song, *I Got Rhythm*

❏ the opening tom tom/piano introduction provides the springboard for startling unison playing between Parker and Gillespie

❏ the melody line of *Shaw 'Nuff* sounds like an improvisation; however, since both Gillespie and Parker were playing the line in unison, that part of the music was obviously pre-planned

❏ Gillespie & Parker show their technical virtuosity with rapid-fire, complex, dense improvisations

❏ Big Sid Catlett's drumming patterns are quite syncopated and not very danceable featuring lots of "punches" and "jabs" rather than consistent backbeat patterns

Example 41

CHARLIE PARKER'S REBOPPERS

KoKo - (1945 New York)
from the album boxed-set, *The Smithsonian Collection of Classic Jazz*

featured musicians:
Charlie Parker - alto sax
Dizzie Gillespie - trumpet / piano
Curly Russell - bass
Max Roach - drums

Recording Notes

❏ the same band members as in Dizzy Gillespie's All-Star Quintet, minus pianist Al Haig

❏ new melody composed by Parker over the form and structure of the popular song *Cherokee*

❏ as in *Shaw 'Nuff,* a startling unison melodic line played by Gillespie and Parker

❏ virtuosic improvisations by Gillespie and Parker

❏ complex, syncopated drum solo by Max Roach; try tapping your foot to this one!

❏ amazingly, the band comes in together at the conclusion of the drum solo because Roach was improvising over the A-A-B-A form of the tune (common popular song structure)

Example 42

CHARLIE PARKER QUINTET

Ornithology - (1948, live - Royal Roost Club, New York City)
from the Jazz Classics album, *Broadcast Performance*

featured musicians:
Charlie Parker - alto sax
Miles Davis - trumpet
Tadd Dameron - piano
Curly Russell - bass
Max Roach - drums

Recording Notes

❏ one of Parker's most famous melodies, *Ornithology* was composed over the form and structure of the popular song *How High The Moon*
❏ live club performance demonstrates the loose, jam session approach of bebop
❏ Parker's solo is quite angular, although performed nearly effortlessly
❏ notice Parker's use of pop tune "quotes" within his improvisation (e.g., *Jingle Bells*)
❏ Davis's solo is not as outgoing as Parker's; more reflective in nature; Davis's playing did not fit the mold of the typical bebopper
❏ Parker and Davis "trade 4's"; an outgrowth of the cutting contests seldom heard in studio recordings of bebop, but always present in live performances

Example 43

CHARLIE PARKER AND STRINGS

Just Friends - (1949, New York)
from the Verve album, *Charlie Parker with Strings*

featured musicians:
Charlie Parker - alto sax
Stan Freeman - piano
Ray Brown - bass
Vernon Brown - trombone
Buddy Rich - drums

Recording Notes

❏ Parker enjoyed going to the symphony and he especially liked the music of Igor Stravinsky (*The Rite of Spring, Petrushka,* etc.)

❏ this was an attempt by his new record company, Verve, to expand his audience by adding strings and harp

❏ while the sound of the recording seems over-produced, Bird's improvisation soars above the saccharine; some critics and musicians consider *Just Friends* one of his masterpieces

Example 44

DEXTER GORDON QUARTET

Bikini - (1947, Hollywood, California)
from the album boxed-set, *The Smithsonian Collection of Classic Jazz*

featured musicians:
Dexter Gordon - tenor sax
Jimmy Bunn - piano
Red Callender - bass
Chuck Thompson - drums

Recording Notes

❑ west coast bebop; Dexter Gordon was based in Los Angeles whereas the primary bebop players were located in New York

❑ the form and structure of *Bikini* is unique: A - A - B - A

- the A sections are all 12-bar minor blues
- the B section is an 8-bar contrasting phrase
- the tune is 44 bars long - a very unusual length providing a challenge for soloists

❑ the tune's name was a political statement against U.S. atom bomb tests in the Pacific Bikini Islands during the post World War II years

❑ notice Gordon's big, full-rounded saxophone tone modeled after Coleman Hawkins

❑ Gordon's improvisation is classic bebop featuring long, flowing lines contrasted with shorter, syncopated phrases

Example 45

THELONIOUS MONK QUINTET

Criss Cross - (1951, New York)
from the album boxed-set, *The Smithsonian Collection of Classic Jazz*

featured musicians:
Thelonious Monk - piano
Milt Jackson - vibes
Sahib Shihab - tenor sax
Al McKibbon - bass
Art Blakey - drums

Recording Notes

❏ original, unusual Monk composition featuring a very angular, syncopated melody line
❏ melody is based upon a typical bebop lick that Monk dismembers and reorganizes by rhythmic displacement (odd phrasing technique) and melodic variation
❏ harmonic movement is erratic and non-traditional
❏ Jackson and Shihab negotiate the structure and harmony of *Criss Cross* quite well in their respective solos (this is a very difficult piece to improvise on)
❏ Monk's solo is perfectly formed around the opening lick of the tune, exploring all of its inner and outer edges, melodically, harmonically and rhythmically

Example 46

THELONIOUS MONK

I Should Care (1957, New York)
from the album boxed-set, *The Smithsonian Collection of Classic Jazz*

featured musician:
Thelonious Monk - solo piano

Recording Notes

❏ an abstract musical painting; all original musical elements are distorted (as are shapes in an abstract painting)
❏ Monk explores the concept of creating tension without release by:

  ■ using exaggerated rhythms
  ■ employing unusual harmonies
  ■ incorporating dissonance
  ■ utilizing unorthodox playing techniques (special effects)

❏ the original tune is purposely and completely distorted
❏ this recording helped pave the way for the free jazz revolution that occurred in the 1960's

Example 47

BUD POWELL TRIO

Somebody Loves Me - (1947, New York)
from the album boxed-set, *The Smithsonian Collection of Classic Jazz*

featured musicians:
Bud Powell - piano
Curly Russell - bass
Max Roach - drums

Recording Notes

❑ this recording displays two different aspects of Powell's playing:

- opening (and closing) chorus: locked-hands technique
- improvisation: single-line, horn-like melodies with sporadic left hand accompaniment

❑ notice how Powell attempts to make his improvised lines horn-like using Charlie Parker as his model
❑ bassist Curly Russell assumes more harmonic and time-keeping responsibilities:

- walking bass lines: formerly left hand activities of the stride pianist
- walking lines outline the harmony as well as providing the four-beat rhythmic pulse and drive of the tune

8. Cool Jazz (and West Coast Style)

Example 48

MILES DAVIS NONET

Boplicity - (1949, New York)
from the Capitol album, *The Complete Birth of the Cool*

featured musicians:
Miles Davis - trumpet
Lee Konitz - alto sax
Gerry Mulligan - baritone sax
John Lewis - piano
Gil Evans - arranger

Recording Notes

❑ arranged by Gil Evans - extension of Ellington's style

- ■ use of complex chords (11ths, 13ths, ♭5ths, etc.)
- ■ cross-section voicings

❑ understated, reflective, "cool" quality in the music
❑ improvised lines come from bebop
❑ composed lines come from Debussy, Ravel, and Ellington
❑ use of composed counterpoint lines
❑ rhythmically less syncopated and more predictable than bebop

....

"Superbly constructed and executed, this score by Evans culminates in a delightful interplay between Davis and the shifting ensemble variations."
—Simon Korteweg, liner notes to *The Complete Birth Of The Cool*

....

Example 49

DAVE BRUBECK OCTET

The Way You Look Tonight - (1946, Oakland, CA)
from the Fantasy album, *The Dave Brubeck Octet*

featured musicians:
Dave Brubeck - piano, arranger
Paul Desmond - alto sax
Bill Smith - clarinet, tenor sax
Cal Tjader - drums

Recording Notes

❏ this was an arranging assignment for Brubeck in a music composition class being taught by famed composer Darius Milhaud at Mills College in Oakland, Ca.

❏ recorded in the basement of the Mills College Music Building

❏ features the use of written counterpoint (multiple, simultaneous melodies), complex harmonies (Impressionistic 11th's, 13th's, etc.), and bebop improvisations

❏ many of the same innovative musical concepts heard in the 1949 Miles Davis *Birth Of The Cool* recordings were already utilized three years earlier by Darius Milhaud's students including Dave Brubeck

....

"We tried to write arrangements that were interesting as composition, but still reflected the style of the soloist, and left the improvisor free to create."

- Dave Brubeck, May 1956

....

Example 50

DAVE BRUBECK QUARTET

Take Five - (1960, San Francisco)
from the Columbia album, *Time Out*

featured musicians:
Dave Brubeck - piano
Paul Desmond - alto sax
Eugene Wright - bass
Joe Morello - drums

Recording Notes

❏ composed by Paul Desmond
❏ as a player, Desmond took the **Lester Young** saxophone style to the extreme

- breathy, hollow, sensuous tone quality
- lyrical improvisations - use of space
- perfect example of the "cool" sound, Desmond was an extremely popular jazz stylist during his career

❏ Take Five is based upon **5-beats** to a measure: sometimes referred to as an **odd time signature**

- most jazz and popular compositions are based upon 4 (or 2) beats to a measure
- difficult challenge to improvise lines based upon an odd number of beats in a measure

❏ Brubeck plays a constantly repeated **rhythmic ostinato** underneath the melody and improvisations, providing a solid musical base for the musicians to play off of
❏ Morello's odd-time drumming patterns were considered revolutionary at the time; odd-time drum solos were virtually non-existent when this recording was made
❏ curiously, this tune became popular enough with listeners to be listed on the Billboard Top 100 chart (#25, 9/61)

119

Example 51

THE MODERN JAZZ QUARTET
AND BEAUX ARTS STRING QUARTET

Sketch for Jazz Quartet and String Quartet - (1960, New York)
from the Atlantic album, *Third Stream Music*

featured musicians:
John Lewis - piano, composer
Milt Jackson - vibes
Percy Heath - bass
Connie Kay - drums

Recording Notes

❑ a graphic example of third stream jazz: combining jazz and classical musical elements

❑ complex composition by John Lewis who combines classical string quartet music with terrific jazz improvisations

❑ the string quartet is assigned classical elements which weave in and out of the jazz improvisations of Lewis and Jackson

❑ drummer Connie Kay utilizes "concert" percussion instruments such as a triangle and suspended cymbal (played with mallets) in addition to his standard drum kit

❑ the prevailing mood of this music is "cool" - soft, subtle, and understated

❑ jazz takes on a new level of perception; parity with classical music and musicians

••

"Sketch is a successful attempt in which the two idioms (classical and jazz) remain distinct, but compliment each other in a way that heightens the qualities of each."
- Max Harrison, liner notes to *Third Stream Music*

••

Example 52

STAN GETZ AND J.J. JOHNSON

Crazy Rhythm - (1957, live - Chicago Civic Opera House, Chicago)
from the Verve album, *Jazz At The Philharmonic:*
The Stan Getz & J.J. Johnson Set, 1957

featured musicians:
Stan Getz - tenor sax
J.J. Johnson - trombone
Oscar Peterson - piano
Herb Ellis - guitar
Ray Brown - bass
Connie Kay - drums

Recording Notes

❑ although Getz considered himself a bebopper, historians and critics place him in the cool jazz style
❑ this recording reveals the bebop nature of his playing (as well as J.J. Johnson):

- ultra fast, virtuosic improvisations
- aggressive, long flowing lines
- spontaneous, jam session approach to this performance (no "fancy" arrangements)
- trading riffs between Getz and Johnson near the end of the recording - a bebop tradition (cutting contest)

❑ however, closer examination of Getz's playing reveals cool jazz traits:

- softer, lighter saxophone sound - almost airy in a few spots
- more academic solo; not as blues-based as Charlie Parker or Dexter Gordon
- his improvised lines sound like "classical melodies" when compared to Parker

❑ although not perceived on an audio recording, Getz projected a cool attitude on stage; more like a classical musician than a jazz club bebop performer
❑ trombonist J.J. Johnson was the premiere bebop trombonist for many years as evidenced by his virtuosic playing on this recording

9. Bebop to Hard Bop - East Coast Style

Example 53

SONNY ROLLINS, DIZZY GILLESPIE, AND SONNY STITT

I Know That You Know (1957, New York)
from the Verve album, *Sonny Side Up*

featured musicians:
Sonny Rollins - tenor sax
Dizzy Gillespie - trumpet
Sonny Stitt - tenor sax

Recording Notes

- ❏ classic performances by three of the greatest jazz soloists of all-time
- ❏ Sonny Rollins' solo stands out as the highlight of this recording
- ❏ Rollins' improvisation is a study in virtuosic improvising; the band plays **stop time** behind his solo
- ❏ the stop time accents are on primary downbeats giving the listener something easy to grab on to while listening to Rollins' complex improvisation
- ❏ Rollins' solo contains several "honking" blues notes as well as long, flowing bebop phrases; this shows the transition from classic bebop to hard bop

Example 54

HORACE SILVER QUINTET

Sister Sadie (1959, New York)
from the Blue Note album, *The Best of Horace Silver*

featured musicians:
Horace Silver - piano, composer
Blue Mitchell - trumpet
Junior Cook - tenor sax

Recording Notes

❑ **riff tune**; jump band style played by a small group
❑ strong rhythm & blues elements in the tune and in all of the improvisations; background riffs played behind soloists
❑ big band style arrangement:

- ■ trumpet vs. tenor sax (brass pitted against the saxes - Fletcher Henderson)
- ■ well-designed harmony notes between the tenor sax and trumpet (cross-section voicings - Duke Ellington)
- ■ **shout chorus** built around repeated blues riffs (Count Basie/Kansas City jazz)

❑ Silver's solo contains strong **gospel** phrases and melodic ideas
❑ Cook's solo is built almost entirely on the blues scale
❑ notice the strong drum **backbeat** on 2 & 4 (rhythm and blues influence)

Example 55

CANNONBALL ADDERLEY QUINTET

The Work Song (1965, New York)
from the Capitol album, *The Best of Cannonball Adderley*

featured musicians:
Cannonball Adderley - alto sax
Nat Adderley - trumpet
Bobby Timmons - piano
Louis Hayes - drums

Recording Notes

- ❑ old folk song re-arranged by Nat Adderley
- ❑ riff tune; rhythm and blues-influenced performance
- ❑ aggressive, funky blues-laced improvisations (although this is not a blues tune)
- ❑ gospel piano accompaniment figures played by Timmons (inspired by Horace Silver)
- ❑ strong drum backbeats on 2 & 4 - very danceable, "toe-tapping" rhythms
- ❑ virtuosic improvisation by Cannonball; notice complex bursts of notes contrasted by lyrical lines
- ❑ notice Cannonball's outgoing, full, rounded alto sax sound; sometimes mistaken for a tenor sax

Example 56

WES MONTGOMERY AND THE OLIVER NELSON BAND

Naptown Blues (1965, New York)
from the Verve album, *Goin' Out Of My Head*

featured musicians:
Wes Montgomery - guitar
Oliver Nelson - arranger / bandleader
Herbie Hancock - piano
Grady Tate - drums

Recording Notes

❏ riff tune; 12-bar A-A-B blues form
❏ recording mix has the guitar playing above the volume of the big band; easy to do on a recording, more difficult in a live performance
❏ aggressive, horn-like improvisation by Montgomery; lots of rhythm & blues elements
❏ big band arrangement similar to the small group/jump band performance of Sister Sadie by Horace Silver:

  ■ use of **cross-section voicings** by Oliver
  ■ background riffs played underneath Montgomery's solo
  ■ notice the areas of **call and response** between Montgomery and the band
  ■ tutti shout chorus occurs near the end of the piece

❏ notice the **octave voicings** in the latter part of Montgomery's solo
❏ call and response between Montgomery and the band near the end of the recording (part of the shout chorus)

10. Miles Davis

MILES DAVIS QUINTET

The Theme (1955, New York)
from the Prestige album, *Miles - The New Miles Davis Quartet*

featured musicians:
Miles Davis - trumpet
John Coltrane - tenor sax
Red Garland - piano
Paul Chambers - bass
Philly Joe Jones - drums

Recording Notes

❏ representative recording of the famed Classic Quintet
❏ Davis preferred to match himself with a saxophonist who provided a stylistic contrast with himself
❏ John Coltrane was a hard bopper from Philadelphia whose playing was aggressive, outgoing and laced with elements of funk and blues - the opposite of Miles Davis
❏ because of the diverse nature of the two primary soloists, this band appealed to both cool and bop audiences ensuring larger record sales and higher (usually sold-out) concert attendance figures
❏ where Davis reflectively understated his musical ideas, Coltrane drove his solos with complex lines reflecting another approach to jazz improvisation
❏ Garland, Chambers, and Jones tailored their accompaniments and rhythmic conceptions to fit the cool approach of Davis as well as the hard bop style of Coltrane
❏ *The Theme* was played by the group at the end of the evening - a "sign-off" tune
❏ instead of the first soloist being either himself or Coltrane, Davis provided a "twist" by having Chambers play the opening improvisation on the bass - something new to jazz performance

Example 58

MILES DAVIS

Summertime (1957, New York)
from the Columbia album, *Porgy And Bess*

featured musicians:
Miles Davis - trumpet
Gil Evans - guitar
Paul Chambers - bass
Philly Joe Jones - drums
Cannonball Adderley - alto sax (in the sax section)

Recording Notes

❏ a creative example of third stream jazz that works very well, especially since the original score of George Gershwin's opera, *Porgy and Bess,* was laced with blues elements

❏ Evans' arrangement of *Summertime* contains:

- complex substitute chords (changed from Gershwin's original composition)
- beautiful cross-section voicings that perfectly underscore Davis's improvisation
- lush instrumentation that includes French horns, a tuba, and woodwind instruments

❏ Davis's solo is a study in the plaintive cry of the blues - the same musical objective called for by Gershwin in his original opera score

Example 59

MILES DAVIS

Solea - (1960, New York)
from the Columbia album, *Sketches Of Spain*

featured musicians:
Miles Davis - trumpet
Gil Evans - arranger

Recording Notes

❏ another third stream jazz project, this time combining Spanish classical music with jazz
❏ Evans scored the background accompaniment parts for brass, woodwinds, and percussion
❏ *Sketches Of Spain* came about after Miles heard a recording of *Concierto de Aranjuez for Guitar & Orchestra* by Spanish composer Joaquin Rodrigo
❏ Miles has unlimited freedom for melodic development in his improvisation on Solea since the piece is modal and contains only one basic scale and chord
❏ his solo is blues-drenched and quite emotional; very effective against the lush musical background created by Gil Evans
❏ notice the swinging quality of the drum pattern even though it is not an American jazz beat
❏ from the album liner notes:

⋯⋯⋯⋯⋯⋯⋯⋯⋯⋯⋯⋯⋯⋯⋯⋯⋯⋯⋯⋯⋯⋯⋯⋯⋯⋯

"A basic form of flamenco is the Solea, an Andalusian version of soledad (loneliness). Generally, it is a song of longing or lament, like the Afro-American blues.

"Miles performs with a depth of emotion and strength of rhythm that represent a compelling blend of the 'deep song' of flamenco and the cry of the blues."
—Nat Hentoff, liner notes to *Sketches Of Spain*

⋯⋯⋯⋯⋯⋯⋯⋯⋯⋯⋯⋯⋯⋯⋯⋯⋯⋯⋯⋯⋯⋯⋯⋯⋯⋯

❏ Miles was inspired by a line from the Spanish writer Ferran:

"Alas for me! The more I seek my solitude,
the less of it
I find. Whenever I look for it, my
shadow looks with me."

Example 60

MILES DAVIS SEXTET

So What (1959, New York)
from the Columbia album, *Kind Of Blue*

featured musicians:
Miles Davis - trumpet
John Coltrane - tenor sax (first sax soloist)
Cannonball Adderley - alto sax (second sax soloist)
Paul Chambers - bass
Jimmy Cobb - drums
Bill Evans - piano

Recording Notes

❏ *So What* is an A-A-B-A structure based upon two modes:

- **A sections - D Dorian**
- **B section - Eb Dorian**

❏ Instead of the horns playing the melody of *So What*, bassist Paul Chambers plays the melody with the horns accompanying - another Miles Davis musical twist

❏ Bill Evans plays complex voicings of chords based upon D Dorian (or D minor); the harmony does not move, but the voicings suggest chordal movement

❏ Evans also plays close-voiced, **cluster chords** - the sound of cluster chords are very intense and abstract

❏ Miles has more freedom of melodic movement and development without the constraints of standard jazz harmonies and key changes

❏ Coltrane's solo flows along naturally; he experienced the same freedom of musical expression that Miles felt

❏ Adderley, on the other hand, did not find the same feeling in modal playing and soon departed Miles' band to form his own traditional hard bop band; his solo is a study in trying to resolve the lack of harmonic movement in *So What*

Example 61

MILES DAVIS QUINTET

Orbits (1965, New York)
from the Columbia album, *Miles Smiles*

featured musicians:
Miles Davis - trumpet
Wayne Shorter - tenor sax
Herbie Hancock - piano
Ron Carter - bass
Tony Williams - drums

Recording Notes

❑ a combination of modal and free jazz with hard bop tendencies
❑ free jazz elements are evident in the tune (composed by Wayne Shorter) as it weaves in and out of time
❑ improvisations are based upon a single mode
❑ to avoid establishing a key center, Hancock does not play the piano until his solo, about 2/3 of the way through the performance; his solo avoids harmony and is a single-line horn-like improvisation
❑ notice how each soloist "quotes" the opening melody at the end of their solos in order to cue the band; this was necessary communication since the improvisations were free-form
❑ listen to the linear style drumming of **Tony Williams**:

■ polyrhythmic (4 independent rhythms occurring simultaneously - one for each limb)
■ direct interaction with the soloist - not simply keeping time
■ lots of cymbal playing - textural contribution to the music

11. John Coltrane

Example 62

JOHN COLTRANE QUARTET

Giant Steps - (1959, New York)
from the Atlantic album, *Giant Steps*

featured musicians:
John Coltrane - tenor sax
Tommy Flanagan - piano
Paul Chambers - bass
Art Taylor - drums

Recording Notes

❏ *Giant Steps* represents the ultimate challenge in harmonic complexity for jazz musicians; Coltrane composed this piece as an exercise in negotiating difficult key changes while improvising

❏ *Giant Steps* represents Coltrane's "good-bye" to hard bop; shortly after this recording was made, he encountered modal jazz as a member of Miles Davis's band on *Kind Of Blue*

❏ Coltrane's solo weaves effortlessly in and out of the rapidly changing harmonies; truly, a virtuosic performance

❏ pianist Tommy Flanagan did not have such an easy time of it; his solo is tentative, and he eventually loses his place in the music only to be "rescued" by Coltrane's re-entrance (and Art Taylor's misplaced drum fill)

Example 63

JOHN COLTRANE QUARTET

My Favorite Things - (1960, New York)
from the Atlantic album, *My Favorite Things*

featured musicians:
John Coltrane - soprano sax
McCoy Tyner - piano
Jimmy Garrison - bass
Elvin Jones - drums

Recording Notes

❏ beboppers established the practice of composing new, complex melodies over the existing forms and harmonies of popular songs

❏ in **My Favorite Things, Coltrane changed the form and harmonies of the song and retained the original melody**

❏ instead of improvising over the original form and harmony, Coltrane established a single mode (one basic chord) and a free form as a basis for improvisation

❏ Coltrane played the original melody at the beginning and the end of the piece over the top of the mode

❏ Unlike Bill Evans (pianist with Miles Davis on *So What*) who used cluster chords and tight voicings, McCoy Tyner played **open chord voicings** - a different sound (sometimes referred to as **"stacked" 4ths or 5ths**)

❏ Coltrane began using the **soprano sax**; attracted to its exotic sound, Coltrane popularized its use in the 1960's

Example 64

JOHN COLTRANE QUARTET

The Promise - (1963, live - Birdland, New York City)
from the Impulse album, *Live At Birdland*

featured musicians:
John Coltrane - soprano sax
McCoy Tyner - piano
Jimmy Garrison - bass
Elvin Jones - drums

Recording Notes

- ❏ recorded live at the Birdland jazz club in New York
- ❏ notice the noisy background and slightly out-of-tune piano that the musicians had to endure (typical playing conditions in jazz clubs)
- ❏ modal jazz composition; freedom of melodic expression
- ❏ free-form improvisations; soloists cue the band at the end of their improvisations
- ❏ representative example of the musical characteristics of this famous quartet:

  - ■ Tyner - open chords, percussive approach
  - ■ Garrison - strong, interactive bass lines: timekeeping responsibilities
  - ■ Jones - linear, polyrythmic drumming patterns; aggressive playing style

- ❏ Coltrane's playing exhibits:

  - ■ climbing, scale-like runs (the sweep)
  - ■ expressive, bluesy bent notes (the cry)
  - ■ sheets of sound - increasing as the solo expands

- ❏ combined modal and free jazz improvisation techniques employed by Coltrane and Tyner

Example 65

JOHN COLTRANE QUARTET

Number One - (1967, New York)
from the Impulse album, *Jupiter Variation*

featured musicians:
John Coltrane - tenor sax
Alice Coltrane - piano
Jimmy Garrison - bass
Rashied Ali - drums

Recording Notes

❏ collective improvisation between all members of the group
❏ textural improvisation instead of melodic
❏ undercurrent of activity by the drums and bass - traditional time-keeping roles abandoned
❏ Alice Coltrane plays the piano texturally, carefully avoiding traditional melodies and harmonies
❏ Coltrane's solo represents FREEDOM - the "buzzword" of the turbulent 1960's

■ **sheets of sound** - angry bursts of notes (Coltrane was making political statements in his music)
■ **the sweep** - sweeping runs up and down the entire range of the tenor sax
■ **the cry** - ultra-high shrieks and wailing sounds

12. Avant-Gard / Free Jazz Styles

Example 66

CHARLES MINGUS

Hora Decubitus - (1963, New York)
from the album boxed-set, *The Smithsonian Collection of Classic Jazz*

featured musicians:
Charles Mingus - bass, composer
Brooker Ervin - tenor sax (1st sax solo)
Eric Dolphy - alto sax (2nd sax solo)
Richard Williams - trumpet

Recording Notes

❑ hard driving, swinging, 12-bar blues hard bop tune with musical twists

- ■ at times, played in two keys at once **(polytonal)**
- ■ riff tune; some of the arrangement was improvised at the recording session (a throwback to the Kansas City big band style)
- ■ riffs are layered on top of each other (another Kansas City big band characteristic)
- ■ brass pitted against the saxes (Fletcher Henderson arranging technique)

❑ three soloists are stylistically quite different from each other:

- ■ **Brooker Ervin** plays exclusively within the blues scale; **rhythm & blues** style
- ■ **Eric Dolphy's** solo is obviously rooted in **free jazz;** his solo flows freely, textural in nature, mostly ignoring the tune's harmonic structure
- ■ **Richard Williams'** trumpet solo is "straight-ahead" **hard bop**

❑ Mingus's walking bass provides the driving energy behind this recording

Example 67

ORNETTE COLEMAN DOUBLE QUARTET

Free Jazz - (1960, New York)
from the album boxed-set, *The Smithsonian Collection of Classic Jazz*

featured musicians:

quartet #1	quartet #2
Ornette Coleman - alto sax	**Eric Dolphy** - bass clarinet
Freddie Hubbard - trumpet	**Don Cherry** - trumpet
Charlie Haden - bass	**Scott LaFaro** - bass
Billie Higgins - drums	**Ed Blackwell** - drums

Recording Notes

❑ *Free Jazz* is one, long free improvisation that takes up both sides of the original LP
❑ composed melodic line: cued by Coleman and played by the four horn players at various points in the piece
❑ solo improvisation emphasized; free of traditional bebop clichés
❑ collective textural improvisation utilized behind the soloist, creating a "sound palate" for the soloist to improvise on
❑ use of background riffs behind the soloist
❑ piano omitted to avoid creating key centers and traditional harmonies
❑ two rhythm sections employed:

1. one drummer & bassist provide traditional walking bass lines and swinging drum patterns
2. the other drummer and bassist create an undercurrent of textural activity and interact directly with the soloist

Example 68

CECIL TAYLOR UNIT

Enter Evening (1966, New York)
from the Blue Note album, *Unit Structures*

instrumentation used:
Cecil Taylor - piano / composer
Instrumentation: oboe, alto sax, bass clarinet, trumpet,
cello, string bass, triangle, cymbal

Recording Notes

❑ Taylor's composition involves composed fragments interjected inside the collective improvisation by the ensemble
❑ *Enter Evening* is a tone poem - the music evokes the sounds heard at dusk
❑ avoidance of most traditional jazz elements; *Enter Evening* stretches the boundaries of jazz
❑ the piece develops gradually, slowly adding thicker sound textures and longer musical phrases
❑ listen for a wide variety of sound textures - the outstanding characteristic of the piece
❑ also listen for bits and pieces of jazz phrasing and other jazz elements that emerge from the sound textures

....

"In *Enter Evening*, the music itself seems to be entering."
—James McCalla, jazz author and critic

....

Example 69

CECIL TAYLOR

Jitney #2 - (1974, live - Montreaux Jazz Festival, Montreaux, Switzerland)
from the Sony/Jazz Classics album, *Jazz Styles: History and Analysis*

featured musician:
Cecil Taylor - solo piano

Recording Notes

❑ one of the few recordings to capture the excitement of Taylor's performances
❑ *Jitney #2* is a spontaneous, free jazz improvisation
❑ textural improvisation - free of bebop melodic clichés and jazz harmonies
❑ turbulent, violent, imaginative performance
❑ to the novice listener, there is a sense of beginning, middle, and end to this piece
❑ Taylor threads his ideas together in such a way that the composition makes sense, even though it doesn't contain traditional jazz elements
❑ notice the reaction of the audience at the conclusion of the performance (compare to the audience reaction of Charlie Parker)

Example 70

THE ART ENSEMBLE OF CHICAGO

Imaginary Situations - (1989, Chicago)
from the *Alternate Express* album

featured musicians:
Lester Bowie - trumpet, percussion
Roscoe Mitchell - flute, African flute, bass clarinet
Joseph Jarman - alto saxophone, percussion
Malachi Favors - percussion, string bass
Don Moye - percussion

Recording Notes

❑ representative example of the free jazz improvisational style of the Art Ensemble of Chicago ("flagship group" of the Association for the Advancement of Creative Musicians - A.A.C.M.)

❑ focus on collective, textural improvisation as well as solo improvisation (everyone gets a short solo)

❑ quieter, reflective improvisations - the equivalent of the "cool side" of free jazz

❑ expanded use of percussion instruments - all of which are exotic instruments not found in traditional jazz (congas, bongos, bells, shakers, log drums, gongs, etc.)

❑ percussion instruments create an undercurrent of activity, textural in nature, rather than traditional time-keeping roles

❑ alto saxophone is played in a non-traditional manner

❑ string bass is bowed instead of plucked

❑ Lester Bowie provides traditional trumpet bebop-influenced melodic lines - the one obvious connection to traditional jazz playing on this recording

Example 71

DAVE HOLLAND QUARTET

Four Winds - (1972, New York)
from the ECM album, *Conference Of The Birds*

featured musicians:
Anthony Braxton - soprano sax (a member of the A.A.C.M.)
Sam Rivers - tenor sax
Dave Holland - bass
Barry Altschul - drums

Recording Notes

❏ the melody of *Four Winds*, composed by Dave Holland, seems almost folk-like in nature with its use of traditional melodic notes
❏ while harmony is implied, it is never formally stated
❏ free-form improvisations are not dependent on traditional harmonic movement
❏ bassist Holland and drummer Altschul weave in and out of traditional time-keeping roles:

- at times, Holland plays traditional walking bass lines; other times he interacts with the horn soloist as a second melodic instrument
- similarly, Altschul plays traditional time-keeping patterns when Holland is walking his bass lines
- at times, Altschul also creates a busy, textural undercurrent of activity

❏ Braxton and Rivers are free to take their improvisations wherever they want; they are not bound by the restrictions of harmonic movement or song structure
❏ the communication between the four musicians is extremely focused:

- Holland & Altschul play "in-time" as well as "out-of-time" as though they were one performer:

"Altschul stuck to Holland like glue."
—Leonard Feather, jazz critic

- Braxton & Rivers not only create virtuosic improvisations, they project a sense of form and structure in their improvisations where none formally exist:

"Anyone who questions whether free jazz music swings, has obviously not listened to the Dave Holland Quartet."
—Leonard Feather, jazz critic

Example 72

KEITH JARRETT

Semblence (1972, Oslo, Norway)
from the ECM album, *Facing You*

featured musician:
Keith Jarrett - solo piano

Recording Notes

❑ spontaneous piano improvisation; the title was added after he recorded the piece

❑ a lyrical melody emerges out of a free introduction and returns near the end of the piece

❑ many different musical styles emerge in his improvised solo including:

- country/folk-like melodic lines
- free-jazz tendencies throughout the solo (some textural exploration)
- a few instances of dissonance contrasted by basic tonal harmony
- classical piano influences and technique
- hard bop phrases
- strong gospel music elements (Horace Silver influence)

❑ very aggressive improvisatory style; the piano equivalent of the sheets of sound saxophone style of John Coltrane

13. Jazz / Rock or Fusion

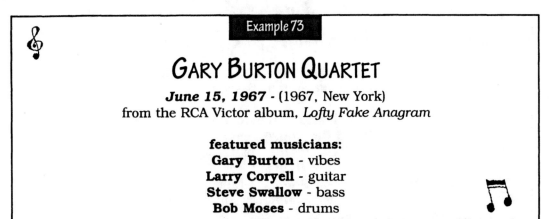

Example 73

GARY BURTON QUARTET

June 15, 1967 - (1967, New York)
from the RCA Victor album, *Lofty Fake Anagram*

featured musicians:
Gary Burton - vibes
Larry Coryell - guitar
Steve Swallow - bass
Bob Moses - drums

Recording Notes

❑ the angular, bebop melodic line of *June 7, 1967*, is set to a straight, non-swinging rhythmic beat
❑ Burton employs gospel elements in his playing that give the vibes a funkier sound
❑ Burton's harmonic approach, however, is deeply rooted in hard bop (he had been playing with Stan Getz and other older jazz musicians just prior to making this recording)
❑ Coryell's guitar sound and style is:

- heavy, on the edge of distortion
- amplified and rooted in rock music
- laced with blues riffs and rock phrases

❑ Coryell's improvisation also contains bebop phrases interjected into his rock style
❑ Bob Moses, a noted hard bop drummer, plays patterns that are rock-based, but generally rooted in the more complex tradition of a jazz drummer (influenced greatly by Tony Williams)
❑ Steve Swallow's acoustic bass provided a link to the sound of bebop, but his lines were rock-based, not traditional walking patterns

---

BLOOD, SWEAT AND TEARS

Example 74

Smiling Phases - (1969, New York)
from the Columbia album, *Blood Sweat And Tears*

featured musicians:
David Clayton Thomas - vocals
Fred Lipsius - piano solo
Dick Halligan - organ
Lew Soloff - trumpet
Bobby Colomby - drums

Recording Notes

❏ vocalist Clayton-Thomas has a rock-sounding voice combined with the phrasing of a jazz singer

❏ while the sound and rhythmic feel of *Smiling Phases* (composed by Steve Winwood) is rock-based, the jazz horns add a new dimension to the overall performance

❏ drummer Bobby Colomby, who had a background in jazz, plays with more sophistication and syncopation than other contemporary rock drummers (inspired by Tony Williams)

❏ the song's rock style evolve into a "straight-ahead," full-blown **hard bop** piano solo by Fred Lipsius during the instrumental break

❏ the brass chorale transition from the jazz piano solo back to the rock vocal suggests an historical connection between the funeral band tradition of New Orleans jazz and its eventual merging with rock music

Example 75

MILES DAVIS

Miles Runs The Voodoo Down - (1969, New York; released, 1970)
from the Columbia album, *Bitches Brew*

featured musicians:
Miles Davis - amplified trumpet
Wayne Shorter - tenor sax
Bennie Maupin - bass clarinet
John McLaughlin - electric guitar*
Chick Corea - electric piano
Larry Young - electric piano*
Harvey Brook - electric bass*
Dave Holland - acoustic bass
Jack DeJohnette - drums
Charles Alias - drums*
* = rock musician

Recording Notes

❑ Miles intended *Bitches Brew* to be one long extended work; the original album was a two-disc, 4-sided release

❑ *Miles Runs The Voodoo Down* is an excellent example from *Bitches Brew*, but does not always project the entire feeling and style of the whole album (just as one song from *Sgt. Pepper's Lonely Hearts Club Band* does not adequately represent that album as a whole)

❑ this segment contains a **modal improvisation** by Miles

❑ his outgoing, aggressive nature during the solo represents a defiance that he directed towards his critics as well as to society in general; Miles was in an angry mood at this point in his career, and his music represents that feeling

❑ as before, the key to his success as an improviser was the connection that he always seemed to make on a human level with his audience; this solo accomplishes that connection

❑ notice the collective, textural improvisations by the electronic keyboards and the bass clarinet going on underneath his solo

❑ the hard-edged sound of the guitar and electric bass are quite evident in this recording - the sound of jazz was changing

"His tone is more vocalized than ever - a human, crying sound. After this quiet start, he develops his ideas with swooping phrases which alternately use the blues scale and then chromaticism. He makes some death-defying forays into the upper register, and his playing is alive with slurs, smears, spaces, screams, long lines, short lines, short tense phrases. It is trumpet playing at a fantastic level, not least for the blazing feeling which he seems barely able to control."
—Ian Carr, 1970 review of *Miles Runs The Voodoo Down* and *Bitches Brew*

Example 76

WEATHER REPORT

Vertical Invader - (1972, live - Shibuya Kokaido Hall, Tokyo, Japan)
from the Columbia album, *I Sing The Body Electric*

featured musicians:
Wayne Shorter - tenor sax
Joe Zawinul - electric piano
Miroslav Vitous - amplified acoustic bass
Eric Gravett - drums
Dom Um Romao - percussion

Recording Notes

❏ live recording captured the energy of the performers and the sold-out audience response

❏ this recording captured the essence of early fusion:

- free jazz improvisation
- performed by jazz-based musicians
- use of electric rock instruments
- heavy amplification and use of distortion electronics
- loud, heavy, driving rock drumming and percussion
- young, rock-oriented listeners; mostly performed in rock venues

❏ collective, textural, free-form improvisations by Shorter and Zawinul over the top of driving rock rhythms by Gravett, Romao, and Vitous

❏ Zawinul utilizes the electric keyboards as textural instruments; a focus on sound development, rather than melodic development

❏ Shorter also focuses on a textural interaction with Zawinul, but with more of a hard bop edge in his improvisations

❏ notice how Vitous utilizes electronic distortion devices on his heavily amplified string bass:

- wah wah pedal
- fuzz tone

❏ Gravett and Romao drive the band with heavy-handed rock drumming patterns

Example 77

JOHN MCLAUGHLIN AND THE MAHAVISHNU ORCHESTRA

Awakening - (1972, New York)
from the Columbia album, *The Inner Mounting Flame*

featured musicians:
John McLaughlin - electric guitar
Jan Hammer - electric keyboards
Jerry Goodman - amplified violin
Rick Laird - electric bass
Billy Cobham - drums

Recording Notes

❑ angular, bebop melody played in unison by the whole band (tutti)
❑ each member of the band (except bassist Laird) gets a solo improvisation featuring rapid, bebop-based, virtuosic melodic lines
❑ improvisations are based on a single mode
❑ Goodman's highly-amplified violin projects:

■ the texture and weightiness of a rock guitar sound
■ the exotic nature of an Indian instrument such as a sarod or sitar

❑ unison melody played as an interlude between each soloist; the melody first appears at the end of each solo improvisation, then it is played by the whole band
❑ Cobham's rock-based drumming also contains strong elements of syncopated bop patterns, especially during his solo
❑ musical tension and sound distortion increase as the melody is played one final time at the end of the performance

Example 78

HERBIE HANCOCK

Watermelon Man - (1973, New York)
from the Columbia album, *Headhunters*

featured musicians:
Herbie Hancock - synthesizers
Bennie Maupin - tenor sax
Paul Jackson - electric bass
Harvey Mason - drums
Bill Summers - percussion

Recording Notes

❑ Hancock originally composed *Watermelon Man* in 1962 and it became a Top 40 hit for Mongo Santamaria

❑ this recording was highly polished, well-produced, and dominated by funk influences

❑ layered rhythms between the synthesizer (guitar-like sound), electric bass, and drums were typical of the funk style established by James Brown, Sly & The Family Stone, George Clinton, and others

❑ Hancock used the synthesizer **orchestrally:** traditional accompaniment role rather than textural sound effects

❑ this recording does not focus on spontaneous, free-form improvisation; rather, the focus is on tight-knit, coordinated ensemble playing (another characteristic of funk)

❑ Hancock conceived the recording itself to be the art form, not necessarily the musical performances contained within the recording - a profound change in the role that recordings served in jazz

Example 79

WEATHER REPORT

Birdland - (1976, New York)
from the Columbia album, *Heavy Weather*

featured musicians:
Wayne Shorter - tenor sax
Joe Zawinul - synthesizers, piano
Jaco Pastorius - electric bass
Alex Acuña - drums

Recording Notes

❑ a musical tribute to the famous New York jazz nightclub named in honor of Charlie Parker: a recognition of past traditions - a new attitude for fusion players
❑ notice the guitar-like melody played by Jaco Pastorius on the electric bass:

    1. use of harmonics (classical guitar playing technique)
    2. electronics, such as octave dividers and phase shifters (technology)

❑ tight, well-produced recording; spontaneous improvisations compromised in favor of a well-rehearsed sound
❑ Birdland is a riff tune; Alex Acuña's drumming pattern is a repeated riff rhythm
❑ synthesizers used orchestrally, rather than texturally
❑ Zawinul also used the acoustic piano to create a more traditional sound
❑ Shorter's solo is relatively short and highly orchestrated
❑ use of contemporary popular elements such as handclaps and electronically modified vocalisms

Example 80

STEPS AHEAD

Trains - (1987, New York)
from the Elektra album, *Magnetic*

featured musicians:
Michael Brecker - tenor sax / MIDI-controlled digital sampler
Mike Manieri - keyboards
Hiram Bullock - guitar
Kenny Kirkland - synthesizers
Victor Bailey - bass
Peter Erskine - drums

Recording Notes

❑ high-energy, techno-flavored fusion performance
❑ very strong drum backbeat played by Erskine: a throwback to the work song tools of labor backbeat of 150 years ago
❑ Brecker's improvisation contains strong references to John Coltrane:

- long, sweeping lines from the bottom to the top of the tenor sax range
- high register "cry" - squeezing out the notes
- rapid, virtuosic bursts of notes
- sheets of sound approach
- big, aggressive, full-tone sound

❑ Brecker's use of digital / MIDI technology is stunning, especially when he plays three-part block harmony with himself near the end of his solo

152

Example 81

MILES DAVIS

Blow - (1991, New York)
from the Warner Brothers album, *Doo Bop*

featured musicians:
Miles Davis - trumpet
Easy Mo Bee - synthesizers / rap vocal

Recording Notes

❑ the merging of jazz and hip hop, popular in the mid-1990's, was originally inspired by this 1991 recording from the Miles davis album, *Doo-Bop*

❑ Easy Mo Bee's rap is rooted in the black culture tradition of **toasting** a member of the community - praising someone in rhyme for their accomplishments

❑ Easy Mo Bee utilizes a sample of *Give It Up Or Turn It Loose* by James Brown as a basis for constructing the tune Blow

❑ despite the technology, the unmistakable sound of Miles Davis cuts through:

- ■ muted trumpet, well-constructed melodic lines
- ■ dramatic use of space

❑ the basic premise of *Blow* is just that: a vehicle for Miles to "blow on" (improvise on)

❑ Miles' improvisation is free-form, modal-based

153

14. Neoclassicism and Post-Modern Bop

> ### Example 82
>
> ## WYNTON MARSALIS
>
> ***Delfeayo's Dilemma*** - (1986, New York)
> from the Columbia album, *Black Codes (From The Underground)*
>
> **featured musicians:**
> **Wynton Marsalis** - trumpet
> **Marcus Roberts** - piano
> **Robert Leslie Hurst III** - bass
> **Jeff "Tain" Watts** - drums

Recording Notes

❑ this recording demonstrates all of the **neoclassic** elements that characterize most of Marsalis' improvisations:

- bravura trumpet sound
- virtuosic technique
- acoustic playing - bebop-based lines
- modal jazz improvisation
- carefully-constructed and dramatically-timed solos
- driving, loose swinging quality - "old school" bop

❑ traditional bebop performance:

- melody (head)
- individual solos (improvisations)
- melody (head)

❑ rhythm section uses the Hancock - Carter - Williams 1960's Miles Davis rhythm section as their model:

- open harmonies played by Roberts on the piano
- occasional *melodic interaction* between Marsalis, the soloist, and Roberts, the accompanist
- linear, polyrhythmic drumming - in the style of Tony Williams, 20 years earlier

Example 83

Joshua Redman Trio

Trinkle Tinkle - (1992, New York)
from the Warner Brothers album, *Joshua Redman*

featured musicians:
Joshua Redman - tenor saxophone
Christian McBride - bass
Clarence Penn - drums

Recording Notes

❑ the lack of a piano does not pose a problem for either Redman or listeners as his solo cleverly outlines the form and harmony of this famous **Thelonius Monk** composition

❑ Redman's improvisation contains hard bop, blues-oriented melodic fragments contrasted with longer, flowing lines

❑ occasionally, he bends and scoops notes, or "honks out" a low tone in the manner of Sonny Rollins and/or Cannonball Adderley

❑ towards the end of his solo, he experiments with sound textures (squeaks and squawks), before concluding with a final bop-based line

Bibliography

ALBERTSON, Chris and John S. Wilson. *Louis Armstrong*. Alexandria Virginia: Time-Life Books, 1978. (book included with the Time-Life Recording, *Louis Armstrong*, STL-J01)

ARMSTRONG, Louis. *My Life In New Orleans*. New York: Prentice Hall, 1954.

BAKER, David. *Jazz Pedagogy*. Van Nuys, California: Alfred Music, 1979.

BARRON, Stanley. *Benny, King Of Swing*. New York: William Morrow And Company, 1979.

BERENDT, Joachim E., revised by Gunther Huesmann. *The Jazz Book: From Ragtime To Fusion And Beyond*. Brooklyn, N.Y.: Lawrence Hill Books, 1992.

BIRNBAUM, Larry. "Art Ensemble Of Chicago: 15 Years Of Great Black Music,' in *Downbeat Magazine*, May 3, 1979.

BROWN, Charles T. *The Jazz Experience*. Dubuque, IA.: W.C. Brown, 1989.

CARR, Ian. *Miles Davis*. New York: William Morrow, 1982.

CHILTON, John. *Who's Who Of Jazz*. New York: Da Capo Press, 1985.

COLE, Bill. *John Coltrane*. New York: Schirmer Books, 1976.

COLE, Bill. *Miles Davis*. New York: William Morris And Company, 1976.

COKER, Jerry. *Listening To Jazz*. Englewood Cliffs, N.J.: Prentice Hall, 1978.

COLLIER, James Lincoln. *The Making Of Jazz*. Boston: Houghton-Mifflin, 1978.

COLLIER, James Lincoln. *Louis Armstrong, An American Genius*. New York: Oxford University Press, 1983.

CROW, Bill. *Jazz Anecdotes*. New Tork: Oxford University Press, 1990.

DANCE, Stanley and Dan Morgenstern. *Duke Ellington*. Alexandria Virginia: Time-Life Books, 1978. (book included with the Time-Life Recording, *Duke Ellington*, STL-J02)

DANCE, Stanley and Richard Sudhalter. *Count Basie*. Alexandria Virginia: Time-Life Books, 1982. (book included with the Time-Life Recording, *Count Basie*, STL-J22)

DAVIS, Francis. *In The Moment: Jazz In The 1980's*. New York: Oxford University Press, 1986.

DAVIS, Miles and Quincy Troupe. *Miles*. New York: Simon and Schuster, 1989.

DUNNING, George. "Impressions Of Art Tatum At The Grand Piano," in *Downbeat Magazine*, October, 1935.

ELLINGTON, Duke. *Music Is My Mistress*. Garden City, N.Y.: Doubleday, 1973.

EWING, Annemarie. "Carnegie Hall Gets First Taste Of Swing," in *Downbeat Magazine*, February, 1938.

FEATHER, Leonard. *The New Encyclopedia Of Jazz*. New York: Bonanza, 1960.

FEATHER, Leonard. *The Encyclopedia Of Jazz In The Sixties.* New York: Horizon, 1966.

FEATHER, Leonard. *The Encyclopedia Of Jazz In The Seventies.* New York: Bonanza, 1976.

FOX, Charles. *The Jazz Scene.* London: Hamlyn Publishing Group, Ltd., 1972.

GIDDINS, Gary. *Satchmo.* New York: Doubleday, 1988.

GILLESPIE, Dizzy. *To Be Or Not To Bop.* Garden City, N.Y.: Doubleday, 1979.

GITLER, Ira. *Jazz Masters Of The Forties.* New York: Macmillan Company, 1966.

GITLER, Ira. *Swing To Bop.* New York: Oxford University Press, 1986.

GLEASON, Ralph J. "Charlie Mingus: A Thinking Musician," in *Downbeat Magazine,* June 1, 1951.

GOTTLIEB, Bill. "Thelonius Monk - Genius Of Bop." in *Downbeat Magazine.* September 24, 1947.

GRIDLEY, Mark. *Jazz Styles: Sixth Edition.* Englewood Cliffs, N.J.: Prentice Hall, 1996.

GROSZ, Marty and Lawrence Cohn. *The Guitarists.* Alexandria Virginia: Time-Life Books, 1980. (book included with the Time-Life Recording, *The Guitarists,* STL-J12)

HAMMOND, John. "Kansas City: A Hotbed For Fine Swing Musicians", from *Downbeat Magazine,* September 1936.

HENTOFF, Nat. "Miles: A Trumpeter In The Midst Of A Big Comeback Makes A Very Frank Appraisal Of Today's Jazz Scene," in *Downbeat Magazine,* November 2, 1955.

HENTOFF, Nat. "Sonny Rollins," in *Downbeat Magazine,* November 28, 1956.

HENTOFF, Nat. "The Birth Of The Cool," in *Downbeat Magazine,* May 2, 1957.

JONES, LeRoi. *Blues People.* New York: William Morrow And Company, 1963.

JOST, Ekkehard. *Free Jazz.* New York: Da Capo Press, 1975.

KAPPLER, Frank A. and George T. Simon. *Benny Goodman.* Alexandria Virginia: Time-Life Books, 1979. (book included with the Time-Life Recording, *Benny Goodman,* STL-J05)

KEEPNEWS, Orrin and Bill Grauer Jr. *A Pictorial History Of Jazz.* New York: Crown Publishers, 1957.

KENNEY, William Howland. *Chicago Jazz: A Cultural History, 1904-1930.* New York: Oxford University Press, 1993.

LANGE, Art. "The Keith Jarrett Interview," in *Downbeat Magazine,* June, 1984.

LISKA, James. "Wynton And Branford Marsalis: A Common Understanding," in *Downbeat Magazine,* December, 1982.

MARTIN, Henry. *Enjoying Jazz.* New York: Schirmer Books, 1986.

McCALLA, James. *Jazz: A Listener's Guide.* Englewood Cliffs, N.J.: Prentice Hall, 1994.

MEGILL, David W. and Paul O. Tanner. *Jazz Issues: A Critical History.* Dubuque, IA: Brown And Benchmark Publishers, 1993.

MEGILL, Donald D., Richard Demory. *Introduction To Jazz History: 3rd Edition.* Englewood Cliffs, N.J.: Prentice Hall, 1993.

MORGENSTERN, Dan. *Jazz People.* New York: Abrams Press, 1976.

MORGENSTERN, Dan. "Weather Report: Outlook Bright And Sunny," in *Downbeat Magazine,* May 27, 1971.

OAKLEY, H.M. "Goodman's Playing Defies Adequate Description," in *Downbeat Magazine,* August, 1935.

OWENS, Thomas. *Bebop: The Music And Its Players.* New York: Oxford University Press, 1995.

PORTER, Louis, Michael ULLMAN. *Jazz, From Its Origins To The Present.* Englewood Cliffs, N.J.: Prentice-Hall, 1993.

PRENDERGAST, Curtis and Richard Sudhalter. *Bix Beiderbecke.* Alexandria Virginia: Time-Life Books, 1979. (book included with the Time-Life Recording, *Bix Beiderbecke,* STL-J04)

REEVES, Scott D. *Creative Jazz Improvisation, 2nd Edition.* Englewood Cliffs, N.J.: Prentice Hall, 1995.

REISNER, Robert G. *Bird: The Legend Of Charlie Parker.* New York: Da Capo Press, 1975.

ROSENTHAL, David H. *Hard Bop: Jazz And Black Music, 1955-1965.* New York: Oxford University Press, 1992.

SCHULLER, Gunther. *Early Jazz: Its Roots And Musical Development.* New York: University Press, 1968.

SCHULLER, Gunther. *The Swing Era: The Development Of Jazz. 1930-1945.* New York: Oxford University Press, 1989.

SHAPIRO, Nat and Nat Hentoff, eds. *Hear Me Talkin' To Ya.* New York: W.W. Norton and Company, 1971.

SHARP, David, Randall Snyder, and Jon J. Hischke. *An Outline History Of American Jazz.* Dubuque, IA: Kendall-Hunt, 1995.

SIMON, George T. *The Big Bands.* New York: The Macmillan Company, 1967.

SOUTHERN, Eileen. *Music Of Black Americans.* New York: W.W. Norton And Company, 1971.

STEARNS, Marshall. *The Story Of Jazz.* London: Oxford University Press, 1958.

SUDHALTER, Richard M., Philip R. Evans, and William Dean Wyatt. *Bix, Man And Legend.* New York: Schirmer Books, 1974.

SWENSEN, John. *The Rolling Stone Jazz Record Guide.* New York: Random House, 1985.

TANNER, Paul, David MEGILL, Maurice GEROW. *Jazz.* Dubuque, IA: W.C. Brown, 1992.

TAYLOR, Billy. *Jazz Piano: History And Development.* Dubuque IA: William C. Brown, 1982.

THOMAS, J.C. *Chasin' The Trane.* New York: Doubleday And Company, 1975.

TIRRO, Frank. *Jazz: A History.* New York: W.W. Norton and Co., 19

TYNAN, John. "Ornette: The First Beginning," in *Downbeat Magazine,* July 21, 1960.

ULANOV, Barry. *Handbook Of Jazz.* New York, Viking Press, 1959.

WHITBURN, Joel. *Top Pop: Singles 1955-1993.* Menomonee Falls, Wisconsin: Record Research, Inc., 1994.

WILLIAMS, Martin. *Jazz Heritage.* New York: Oxford University Press, 1985.

Index

162

Y

Z